PLAN YOUR NOVEL LIKE A PRO

A PRO

And Have Fun Doing It!

BETH BARANY

EZRA BARANY

PLAN YOUR NOVEL LIKE A PRO: AND HAVE FUN DOING IT!

c. 2018 Beth Barany and Ezra Barany

WRITER'S FUN ZONE PUBLISHING

771 Kingston Ave., #108

Piedmont, CA 94611

ISBN 978-1-944841-21-8 1st Edition Print

ISBN 978-1-944841-22-5 1st Edition E-Book

BARANY SCHOOL OF FICTION SERIES

More Barany School of Fiction resources at
BaranySchoolofFiction.com

For bulk orders, contact orders@writersfunzonepublishing.com.

 Created with Vellum

Contents

This book is for all writers who want to bring their stories out into the world.

Introduction & Essential Tips

Introduction

"Writing a novel isn't easy. If it were, everyone would be doing it." —Anonymous

It's your dream to be a novelist, to touch readers' hearts and minds, to excite and wow them, to transport them. And to build a career with your books.

But you don't know where to begin. Starting is hard. Things like creating an outline, scenes, or conflict may be confusing or strange or no fun at all. Perhaps crafting compelling three-dimensional characters stumps you.

Or maybe you've been stuck in the middle of writing your first novel (or fifth) for way too long.

That's hard.

We know. As working novelists, we've been there many, many times.

But there is hope.

Who This Book is For

This book is for you if you want to work on your novel while managing the rest of your life. We know you have other activities and people you are committed to. Your life doesn't stop just because you want to create art. You may feel like your daily life is an obstacle, but it can enhance your storytelling.

This book is also for you if you have tried writing without any guidelines but didn't get very far. It can be hard to write when you don't know what you're writing about, how to develop a story, or why your writing means so much to you.

You may have tried planning your novel by following rules set out by other writing teachers and found that they didn't work for you. Some writing instructors insist that their way is the only way, the best way, but in fact, there is no best way. There is only the way that gets you writing and that is different for every writer.

Plan Your Novel Like A Pro is designed to help you discover your very own creative process for planning your novel. The only way you'll uncover what works for you is to experiment with different tools. Try everything, discard what doesn't work for you, and keep what does. We offer plenty of strategies and tools in this book. Above all, this book is for you if you're looking for a way to listen to yourself, whether that's listening to the whispers of your gut, your heart, your intuition, or some other creative part of you.

Plan Your Novel Like A Pro focuses on genre fiction,

genres such as romance, mystery, thrillers, science fiction, and fantasy. We focus on these types of stories since they are the kind both of us (Beth and Ezra) write and know the most about, but we imagine that writers of other kinds of stories will find helpful exercises and advice among these pages.

The Creative Process

Creating art can be hard and frustrating. It may require you to stretch in ways you never have before. We all start in a place of not knowing. Yet, we humans have been creating art for more than 100,000 years, the age of the oldest art found. (Painted on cave walls in Spain. See citation in the Resources section.)

There is hope.

The friction between the desire to create and the challenge of creating assists our art making and is often what allows us to create our best work.

Start with breathing and noticing what you are feeling, whatever those feelings are. It can be healing to allow yourself to notice and feel whatever it is. Feelings are not good or bad, but rivers of energy that flow through our bodies. We can harness those feelings for our storytelling, but only if we feel them first.

Next, take a breath, or several, and appreciate all the work you've done to get to this place. Appreciate your passion, your focus, and your love of story, and whatever else excites you about writing a novel.

Likewise, appreciate the pain, frustration, disappointment, and even hopelessness you've experienced to get to this point. Without the effort, how would you know if the work was worthwhile?

When we appreciate our current experience, what's happening now, we can choose a new present. What new present do you choose?

You can choose by asking: What would I like? Or, what do I want? Perhaps,

- A completed novel that you can hold in your hands?
- A creative process or model you can use again and again?
- An author career you're happy about and proud to be building?

If you said yes to any of these three things, or to something similar, or even if you're not sure what you would like, then you are in the right place. We are here to help you discover your creative process and lay the foundation for your writing goals.

This book is designed to guide you through the process of planning of your novel. It's a road map to follow, so you can focus on creating.

Planning with a Purpose: Stories Matter

"Story evolved as a way to explore our own mind and the mind of others, as a sort of dress rehearsal for the future. As a result, story helps us survive not only in the life-and-death physical sense but also in a life-well-lived social sense." – Lisa Cron, *Wired For Story: The Writer's Guide to Using Brain Science to Hook Readers from the Very First Sentence*

This isn't an ordinary book on novel planning. While it contains many of the ingredients you may have seen in other writing guide books, it's different because we focus on your creative soul, your heart, and your sense of self and story.

The world needs your stories. Your stories matter.

Your readers are waiting for your unique voice. You matter.

Like many writers, you may have been deeply touched by stories told to you or books you read when you were young, and now you want to influence readers yourself.

Stories are how we make sense of the world and prepare for any potential scenario we may face. They are a form of mental rehearsal. They are how we teach life lessons. As Lisa Cron says so aptly, based on neuroscientists' understanding, "humans are wired for story." I'd even say that it's the most powerful way we learn how to be human, how to ask and answer the questions about how we want to live in the world, and how we can shape our world.

Your stories can influence the fate of future generations, the fate of humanity, and the fate of our planet.

Who Are We and Why Listen to Us

This book comes out of the passion of Beth Barany, that's me. I'm the primary voice of this book, though some of the lessons are by my husband, Ezra, who edits everything I write. And vice versa. (Here's a sentence he added in. His edits are everywhere!)

Together, we are both writing teachers and novelists. We walk the talk, always working on a new novel while we do the other things. As of the publication date, Ezra is working on his fifth Torah Codes thriller and I am editing a four-book science fiction mystery series, due out in the fall of 2019.

What This Book is About

In *Plan Your Novel Like A Pro*, Ezra and I will help you think and write through the steps to create your novel —from character development, to plot structure, story themes and world building, and beyond, so you can start writing your novel with confidence.

As a bonus and to support you in taking action, sign up to get the *Plan Your Novel Like A Pro* workbook, and other bonus material, and follow along with the exercises in an organized way:

http://bethb.net/bonusworkbook.

How This Book is Organized

This book's content started as a live workshop, then was a home study course. It was designed to be completed in thirty days. We've kept that structure in this book—four sections, one per week—so that you can schedule your time and complete the planning process in a month, if you like. Or you can go through the book at your own pace, in a shorter or longer timeframe. If you're new to novel writing, I recommend using the thirty-day or four-week structure to create a vessel in which to explore the coves, lagoons, and rivers of your unique story.

Each exercise can be done in fifteen to twenty minutes, although you may want to spend more time on some. If you follow the suggested curriculum, you may spend eight to ten hours over one month to complete the assignments and exercises.

As a warm-up, we start with an overview to give you a broad picture of the process ahead, sharing essential elements of character from my perspective and essential elements of plot from Ezra. Then we begin in earnest with Week One.

In Week One, we help you write the one-to-two sentence story blurb, also known as the elevator pitch, which you can later use in a query letter (the pitch letter to a literary agent or editor.) Next, we cover the five-to-six paragraph story summary that can form the basis of the synopsis that agents, editors, and publishers often request. We also touch on your story's theme, hook, and genre to give you a better idea of the focus of your story and your audience's expectations.

In Week Two, we cover getting to know your main characters. Great stories start with great characters that you love! We give you a tailored questionnaire and special exercises designed to help you become intimate with your characters, so you can bring them to life when you write your novel.

In Week Three, we help you design the story's main plot points and help you get to know the world of your story better, in other words, we help you with world building. Your plot comes from characters, from knowing your story world, and from asking good questions. We will help you design a plot that keeps your readers turning pages deep into the night.

A word about the plot-driven vs. character-driven argument. I've worked with authors who approach storytelling from both angles, and both types of writers write and finish their novels. There is no right way to approach writing your novel, only the way that works for you. If you're not sure which author type you are, then this book will help you discover what approach you prefer, because we give you exercises that allow you to explore both.

In Week Four, we guide you through the final planning step of building your story scene-by-scene. We help you create an organic outline from all the notes and thinking you did in the prior weeks, and also provide tips on a more linear approach to plotting your story.

Once you have completed all these exercises, you'll

have a good sense of your entire story, and you can sit down to write your novel with excitement and confidence.

Though this book gives you a road map to follow, it isn't a paint-by-numbers process. We have created a step-by-step structure, but if you find that the order doesn't work for you, do the steps in any order you would like. Maybe you will come up with the story idea and plot first. In that case, start with Week Four and work backwards. If you prefer to start with your characters, start with Week Two. If you're not sure where to begin, start with the Overview chapter, then move to Week One.

On Judging Your Work Too Soon

As you work through this book, you may wonder if your ideas are "any good." That can stop you from writing, kick you out of your creative flow. I've seen that happen many times. This question is normal, but not yet useful. When in the planning stage, it is too soon in the creative process to judge your ideas. Writers have asked me if their idea is any good, yet they've only uncovered a tiny portion of the story. It's like asking a plant shoot peeking out of the ground if it will be a wonderful tomato plant. There's no way to know, until that plant matures. Same goes for your story. As with gardening, you need patience and compassion in this process, especially at the idea generation stage: brainstorming.

Brainstorming is all about getting out all your

ideas first. The evaluation and analysis processes come later. You can analyze your story outline once it's created. The exercises in *Plan Your Novel Like A Pro* are designed to help you think through your story before you write it. Let yourself have fun with this process.

If you judge your creative work too soon in the brainstorming process, (and especially if you're a beginner), you're not being fair to your muse or your work. Your story needs time to flower and mature into what it is meant to be.

My advice is to invite your judgment to take a walk, go to the mall, or go on a vacation for a bit. I've offered this advice to hundreds of students over the years, and each one who listened has reported that this helped them get words on the page much more easily than if they'd stopped to judge every other word.

Your job now is to show up for the work.

This means putting pen to page or fingers to keyboard or voice to transcription and being present for the story, however you may feel, on good days and bad ones. People often think that their life has to be perfect before they sit down to write. But actually, you can incorporate your current emotional state into your stories and your characters, and it will make your work stronger.

If you have a hard time getting started, set a timer for twenty minutes, or even five, and just write. This is my favorite get-writing tool.

On Learning

This book, and all our trainings at Barany School of Fiction are designed for people who are taking (or who could take or have taken) college-level courses. We assume:

- You know how to ask for help.
- You are responsible for your own education.
- You are learning by various means, one of which is this book.
- You know how to manage your time.
- You know how you learn through your individual combination of reading, writing, listening or watching, and you're in tune with your most effective learning style.

Check out Barany School of Fiction here: https://BaranySchoolofFiction.com.

On Learning How to Write Fiction

"If you want to be a writer, you must do two things above all others: read a lot and write a lot. There's no way around these two things that I'm aware of, no shortcut." – Stephen King

You can learn to write compelling fiction, though it's one of the most challenging forms of writing. It is different from school essays and from most business writing.

There are three things that are essential for becoming a good writer: reading, writing, getting feedback on what you've written.

To write the kind of fiction you want to write you need to read it. All the writers we have ever met who have completed a manuscript are avid readers and fans of the types of stories they write. They usually also read outside of their genre, exploring a wide variety of other kinds of fiction and nonfiction.

To be a writer is to actually do the writing. Because if you don't write, you aren't a writer. And if you don't read, there is no way you could possibly know what your readers are hankering for.

The third essential element is to get feedback on your writing. To get you started, sign up for the Bonus material for some resources on finding or creating a writer's critique group.

What Comes After This Book

Once you have planned your novel, it's time to write! I will recommend next steps for you. While this isn't a book about editing, readers have told me that this book has helped them get unstuck, make revisions, and get writing again.

While planning your novel, you may discover that you want to learn more about the craft of fiction writing. Throughout this book, I offer resources for you to pursue and dive deeper into every topic. I touch on marketplace concerns in this book, but don't cover publishing or marketing at all. Recommended resources for those are in the Resources section at the end of the book.

Sign up for the Bonus Workbook

To help you implement the exercises in this book, sign up for the Bonus Workbook here:

http://bethb.net/bonusworkbook.

ONE

Essential Character Tips for Fiction Writers

*S*o you can get started thinking about your main character right away, I have three essential character tips for when you plan your novel. More tips, tools, and exercises on developing your main and secondary characters are in Week Two.

Tip #1: What Does Your Main Character Want? Their Goals

What does your character want? That's super important. Stories are built on characters and their journey to get what they want. It's up to us authors to put obstacles in the character's way so they can't easily obtain what they want. (Otherwise there would be no story.) Once the roadblocks are built, you'll create a resolution where the character may or may not overcome the obstacle. Usually in genre fiction, you'll create a happy resolution, but you don't have to have a happy ending, of course. It's your story.

Your main character needs to have goals. That includes an external goal—something your main character goes after that is bigger than them. It needs to be enough of a challenge to carry your story, perhaps coming from your character's yearning, and it needs to be relevant for your genre.

For example, I write in several genres, including fantasy, mystery, and romance. In the third book of my epic fantasy series, *Henrietta and the Battle of the Horse Mesa*, I needed to create a big goal for my main character, Henrietta. But first, she had an initial goal, which changed into a big goal that befitted the final book in a series.

My main character's initial goal is to return a six-year-old boy to his mother. A multi-kingdom war is brewing. Henrietta's bigger goal is to decide whether or not she should lead the army, and if she decides yes, then she has to figure out how to do that.

Your main character also needs an internal goal. It could be that they want respect, admiration, or to love and be loved. In my example, Henrietta is not that deep a thinker, but she does want respect. Most importantly, she wants freedom. She has two competing internal desires—one for freedom and the other to do the responsible thing. That's one of her big challenges. I'll get to challenges in a moment. Once you know your character's goal, then you need to know why they want what they want. This will help you get a three-dimensional understanding of your story.

Tip #2: Why Does Your Character Want What They Want? Their Motivation

I find it works best to interview my characters. Ask your character, "Why do you want this thing so badly?"

For example, my question for Henrietta: was, "Why do you want to return the boy Antoine to his people so much?"

This is a very important question to use when uncovering your main character's why. It comes from a discipline of how we humans are motivated. This field is called neuro-linguistic programming or NLP. It's the study of how we grow, learn, and change, and how we can achieve the kinds of goals that we want in life. I studied this as a form of personal development, and as a way to help my clients in my coaching business. I work with authors and found these tools to be so much fun and useful, I applied them to my fictional characters.

The key question to ask your characters, once you have discovered what they deeply want in your story is, "What will having that do for you?" Ask this question with respect to their outer goal and to their inner goal. It is so much fun to interview your characters. I've done this exercise many times with my students and clients, and each of them reports gaining a deeper awareness of what drives their character.

For example, Henrietta wants to deliver the boy, Antoine, to his mother. Through writing I asked, "Henrietta, what will having that do for you?" Her reply: she felt a sense of obligation. To get the full value of asking this question you want to ask it at least three to five times. That way you'll uncover the core motivation.

Then I ask, "You feel a sense of obligation? Once you've delivered the boy, then I guess that sense of obligation will be relieved? Again, what will having that do for you—to deliver the boy to his mother?" Henrietta's reply: She won't be treated like a mother anymore and no longer will have this little boy hanging on her, "Mommy, mommy" She's a seventeen-year-old warrior woman, her whole life in front of her. Time enough to be a mother later, much later.

As much as she's grown attached to him, she doesn't want that responsibility, so she's driven by both a sense of obligation and a desire not to be responsible. Already, I've created some interesting tensions inside her.

I keep asking, "What will having that do for you, once you're relieved of this pretend motherhood?" I discover under that, is a belief she has about herself: "I could never be a mother" Now I understand that she's driven by a rejection of the possibility of motherhood.

I keep going.

"Henrietta, what will having that do for you?"

I discover underneath her sadness, that she really

would love to be a mother and would love to have a family. But because she's a warrior, she doesn't think it's for her. It's more a rule she's made in her head that she can't break.

Just by asking this question again and again, "What will having that do for you?" you can uncover complicated juicy material that motivates your character. This kind of complexity helps us make our characters feel real to our readers.

When you ask, "What will having that do for you?" notice that the replies come from your subconscious where all our stories lie. In my case, these ideas sit in my subconscious and mull with all the other material that I use to develop my character.

So far, we've talked about your character's goals and what motivates them to want those goals. Our first two essential character tips.

Tip #3: What Stands in Your Character's Way: Conflict

The third essential plot tip I want to share with you is about conflict. I approach conflict in an atypical way because I'm a character writer.

I first encountered conflict, or lack thereof, as a writer, when critique partners said to me, "Beth, your characters are so sweet, but you have to make bad things happen to them. Otherwise, you don't have a story."

I had a hard time coming up with conflict that happens outside of my characters. That's not the way my brain works. Through lots of trial and error, I discovered this exercise: asking my character, "What are you afraid of?"

This helped me uncover possible conflicts for my stories. If you know what scares your character, then you can incorporate that into your story as conflict.

As a brainstorming tool, I created this exercise I call the "List of 20."

Here's how I use it: I write the numbers one through twenty on my page—I prefer to handwrite this exercise. Then I set a timer for about ten minutes. This is usually a good amount of time to complete this exercise. Then I list all the fears that my character has. I just move my pen. It's okay if I repeat things. It's okay if there's no discernible order. I just write, write, write.

What I discovered in doing this exercise is that my brain organizes my fears in order of normal or obvious fears into deeper and bigger ones. This doesn't always happen, but there's often a discernible pattern, resembling the outline of a story. Who knew!

The first time I did this exercise, I was super happy and very surprised because I had discovered a way to create a story outline.

A process I had previously rejected, which had always given me the heebie-jeebies. I discovered a way to structure a story by identifying my character's fears.

For example, as I was brainstorming, *Henrietta and the Battle of the Horse Mesa*, Book Three of the *Henrietta The Dragon Slayer* series, in preparation for the upcoming National Novel Writing Month (NaNoW-riMo)*[1], I asked myself, "What are Henrietta's fears?" One of her fears was that she would lose Franc, her companion. At the beginning of the story, they were traveling together, so it was an obvious fear. She cared deeply for him and didn't want their companionship to end. What if something bad happened to him?

I got excited when this fear came to me. "That would be an amazing conflict," I thought. Her fear of losing Franc could occupy a whole section, maybe even the whole book.

Ideas about what she would do if she lost Franc came tumbling in. Since I was drafting my List of 20, and needed to come up with more ideas, I asked myself, "What else is she afraid of? What could be worse than that?" Some other ideas I uncovered: She was afraid of being under the thumb of anyone in authority, so what if she had to ask someone in authority in this new territory for help? That would make finding Franc harder. Good! That's what we want for our characters—for things to get worse before they get better.

But I still didn't have twenty fears. I kept asking, "What else is she afraid of?" She was afraid of looking stupid because she was a smart mouth. She was in a territory that she didn't know, so that was perfect. Everything in her environment could cause her problems. I was stacking the problems, all based on Henrietta's fears. Just those three things right there were super juicy. I was sure I could come up with more.

For this exercise to have maximum benefit, there are a few assumptions to make. One is that you know your genre. You know the kinds of characters that fit in your genre. You know the general goals. You know what would be appropriate for motivating them, and you know their fears.

I have shared with you my three essential character tips for my fantasy character, Henrietta. Now I'll give you another example since the character goals, motivations, and conflicts in romance, are different from epic fantasy. I still use paranormal and magical elements in my romance, but the scale of the story is much smaller.

I was daydreaming a new Christmas elf romance. My character's main goal was to please his father. For this young man, nothing he did in the elf world pleased his father. His latest fiasco was making weird food in the kitchens that are meant to cater to all the elves who make the toys. He was apprenticing in the kitchens because he'd failed everywhere else. He was messing up the food, but in a very creative way. He was combining cranberries and carrots, and gosh, what else? Pistachios and maybe, a little ginger. Instead of green and red sprinkles, he was using white and orange sprinkles. These weren't Christmas colors; he wasn't making Christmas food. His goal was to please his father, but he was failing.

I set up conflict by his behavior, not meeting his goal. This young man needed an outer goal too. In romance, outer goals can take all kinds of forms. In this story, he realized he had to pick a profession.

A Christmas Cupcake started (Book #5, Touchstone Series) with these ideas, which evolved as I brainstormed further and then wrote the book.

What would motivate my elf hero? I discovered that his goal was to please his father, and that was also what motivated him. I asked him, " What will pleasing your father do for you?" Then, I could discover that once he accomplished this, he thought he'd get a golden ticket, which meant he could go off and do whatever he wanted. I asked again, "What will having *that* do for you?" I discovered what he really wanted was freedom. Freedom to have a life however he wanted it, but he didn't quite know this about himself at the beginning of the story.

Again, I asked, in case there was anything more. "What will having that do for you once you have freedom?" He had a big grin on his face. "Then I'll be happy."

That's what we want in our romances, for our characters to be happy. We're creating Happily Ever Afters, after all.

Of course, there's going to be a woman who comes in there and stirs the pot and makes things complicated and better than he could have ever expected.

For conflicts, I already shared a few. He was messing things up for the elves, and he wanted to get out of there. Because he was somebody who was driven by freedom, I gave him conflicts that would restrict him in some way. For example, he wasn't allowed to reveal that he was a Santa's elf in the human world. He had to hide his pointy elf ears and he couldn't use magic. Since this was my second Christmas Elf Romance, those restrictions were already built into my world.

He was afraid of not finding his path. That was fun because of the potential conflicts. What if I put a heroine into the story who absolutely knew her path? Then, something would have to bring them together, maybe working in a cupcake factory or a cupcake boutique restaurant. Maybe she was his boss.

This is how I scenario plan. I come up with ideas, and then I test them with other people. If they don't work, that's okay. I move on to the next one, since that is our job as writers: to keep coming up with new ideas and then make them fit like a wonderful, complicated, beautiful puzzle.

To Recap

These three essential character tips are that you want to uncover your main character's goal, motivation, and conflict. Find these three things for each of your main characters. For the goal, each main character has an inner goal and an outer goal, inner and outer conflicts, plus corresponding motivations for each goal.

Often the goals and their motivations are intertwined. The same is true with conflict. You may have inner conflict like doubt, worry, or fear. Then, you might have outer manifestations of those conflicts. That's another way of looking at goal, motivation, and conflict.

Go Deeper

If you'd like to explore your character further with these three elements—goal, motivation, and conflict—I created an exercise as a useful way to step more into your character and yourself—the source material for all your fiction. Sign up for the workbook to get this exercise. http://bethb.net/bonusworkbook.

For Further Reading

The source material for these three essential tips is *Goal, Motivation and Conflict* from Gryphon Books for Writers by Deb Dixon, available on the Gryphon Books for Writers website:

https://gryphonbooksforwriters.secure-chrislands.com/product/23.

In the Week Two section, we'll go into more tips and tools for developing your characters.

But before that…

Next

Ezra will share his three essential tips for plotting.

---

1. NaNoWriMo stands for National Novel Writing Month and is a wonderful and free worldwide movement to write a 50,000-

word   novel   during   November.   More   details   at https://nanowrimo.org/.

TWO

Essential Plot Tips for Fiction Writers

*E*zra here.

What are the most important parts of your story?

Tip #1: The Most Important Part of Your Story—The End

I would say the most important part of the story is the ending. For example, you can have a wonderful book, but if it has a bad ending, then readers will probably dislike the story. On the flip side if you are really bad at writing (but a great storyteller), and you have a great ending, hey, you'll win! The readers will love that. But then you might ask yourself, "Self, how am I supposed to make sure that I have a great ending?"

Answer: Brainstorm endings with the List of 20.

Beth and I love the List of 20. It's something we use a lot, anytime we need to brainstorm an aspect of our stories.

. . .

ACTION

Set a timer for ten minutes. Have a piece of paper numbered from one to twenty and brainstorm possible ideas. In this case, possible ideas on how your story will end. Sure enough, something will pop up that makes you shiver with delight and you'll say, "That's it!" That's the one you want. This exercise is a great way to come up with a fantastic ending. Try it. You'll like it.

Tip #2: The Second Most Important Part of Your Story: The Beginning

The second most important part of the story is the beginning. You want to hook your reader in. You want to catch the tiger by the toe, and when the reader hollers don't let them go. You hooked them in.

ACTION

Use the List of 20 to brainstorm potential beginnings to find the one that best hooks the reader for the kind of story you're writing.

Tip #3: No deus ex machina

deus ex machina. A person or thing (as in fiction or drama) that appears or is introduced suddenly and unexpectedly and provides a contrived solution to an apparently insoluble difficulty. (merriam-webster.com) A device used in Greek plays, comes from the Latin expression, "a god from the machine." (Wikipedia)

Don't use this device. It drives your readers nuts.

If your hero and heroine, or just the hero, are at their wits end and there's nothing possible to save the day, what's going to happen? God, or maybe a paranormal creature like a ghost, or even some random person walking down the street who happens to have a fix, comes in out of nowhere to save the day. And you've never introduced him before in the story.

That doesn't work. People hate that.

I think the best example of where it actually worked in a story would be the movie, *Raiders of the Lost Ark*. There you have God jumping in, saving the day. I always ask myself, why did that work? I would say the reason it worked in that situation was because God was not a player that popped out of nowhere. First, He was introduced in the explanation of what the Ark is. The Ark was something that the Hebrews carried, and God would present Himself through the Ark and defeat all the enemies. Later on, a foreshadowing, the dropping of clues, took place in the film. The Ark was inside a box and the swastika on the box burned magically. You already had the idea that God was present during all of this.

I'd say in that case, it worked because of the foreshadowing. In my thriller novel *The Torah Codes*, if I had done more foreshadowing it would have been a better story. I got some pretty scolding reviews for my *deus ex machina*.

If you find yourself creating a *deus ex machina*, then brainstorm ways you can foreshadow that element from the very beginning of your story. You can always add foreshadowing back during the editing phase.

Tip #4: Your Story's Dénouement

Dénouement. n. The conclusion or resolution of a plot.

At the end of your story, especially in the case of a thriller or a mystery, the external conflict is over, but still the internal conflict needs to be addressed. It's time to tie up the story's loose ends in one or two scenes or chapters.

In romance, readers want a bit of a longer ending. They want to bask in the happily ever after. At the end, you show your couple coming together, but you also want to show the moment that begins the happily ever after, whether it's a holiday moment or the baby being born, or something lovely like that.

In the fantasy genre, the wrapping up of loose ends is very satisfying to readers, though you may not want to wrap up until the last book if you're writing a series. You still want to end each book skillfully but then hook them for the next one.

How you write your dénouement will depend on your genre.

In my second Torah Codes thriller, *36 Righteous*, I made sure the ending was short and sweet. I did have an extensive ending planned out at first, but I figured out how to cut it, resolve all the issues, and make it as succinct as possible. That was necessary for this story because the climax was a huge surprise, a major twist. We're talking Sixth Sense movie twist.

Knowing that there's this huge surprise ending, I wanted people to leave off with that and not have to read more pages. I wanted to make that ending exciting, and not dilute it by making it longer than it had to be.

Tip #5: Explode That Bomb

"One must not put a loaded rifle on the stage if no one is thinking of firing it." — Anton Chekhov

If there's a bomb in your story, it's got to explode. I'm not talking about an actual bomb. It could be represented by other things in different genres, even romance.

Not having heard of this quote at the time, I was turned on to the concept by a Simpson's TV episode. Itchy and Scratchy were driving in a car and passing signs that read, "Ten miles away from the rocket factory," then "Five miles away from the rocket factory," and so on. They were getting closer and they were getting angrier and angrier at each other. Finally, they resolved their issues and became friends. That was the end. And I wondered, "What about the rocket factory?" I wanted an explosion and I was disappointed.

In the opening of my book *36 Righteous*, two bombs are defused. I left the reader with no explosions, then realized, "No, I can't do that." Something had to explode.

In the case of romance, maybe the hero is coming to stop the heroine from getting married to the wrong man or to the villain, but there has to be a wedding. The readers are expecting that.

Typically, a way to resolve this is to have the thing that's averted—whether it's a bomb exploding or the wedding that is stopped—happen to the other person. The bomb is stopped, so the hero saves the school children, but then the villain finds the bomb in his briefcase. So instead of the school yard exploding, it's the villain. Or the hero stops the wedding from happening so the villain doesn't get married, but then the hero gets to marry the heroine and the wedding is still there.

To Recap

Essential to making my story great, I brainstorm these five things when planning my novel:

- The end
- The beginning
- Foreshadowing to prevent *deus ex machina*
- The dénouement
- Planting and exploding the "bombs"

Bonus Tip: Write crap.

When it comes time to write your novel, write anything, even if it's crap. Get your words on the page. You can always edit them later. It's a lot easier to meet that word count when you're not focused on quality. You'll be surprised at how good it is later on, as long as you're not thinking about making it pristine the first time around. Just get it out there. Pledge to do this, and you'll find that you can write a first draft faster than you think. I've written eight novels, each one during NaNoWriMo. One year, instead of novels, I wrote five short stories.

It's amazing what you can do with some planning and with permission to write crap. Surprise yourself!

NEXT

Beth will start us on Week One and start you on the novel planning with short exercises and small steps: the elevator pitch & short synopsis.

Week One: Elevator Pitch, What-If Pitch & Short Synopsis

THREE

Elevator Pitch

n Week One, Ezra and I will help you write the one-to-two paragraph story blurb, also known as the elevator pitch. Expanding on that, we guide you to draft a five to six paragraph story synopsis. In this section, we also touch on three key aspects of story planning, so that you have a better idea of the focus of your story and your audience's expectations: the story's theme, a story hook called a what-if pitch, and your story's genre.

Like an accordion, this book will help you open up your story little by little. Let's start small and build from there.

ELEVATOR PITCH

Even if you only have the barest inkling of an idea, writing your elevator pitch can help your creative juices flow. It also helps you get greater clarity about what it is you are creating and who specifically your audience is.

An elevator pitch is another name for a book blurb. You see it on the back of books and on an online book record, usually under "Book Description" or "Overview." Consisting of five parts, about two to five sentences, this is one of the shortest representations of your story. I recommend you start with the elevator pitch. It's an activity you can do in five to twenty minutes, and it's a good way to get your brain in gear for writing.

Remember: It doesn't need to be right. It just needs to be written! Don't worry about your elevator pitch being perfect. You can revise it once you're done with all your novel planning or even when you're done writing your novel.

Genre: Start here

To be able to do the exercises in Week One, and in the rest of the book, it's helpful to think about your genre, so that you'll have a general idea of your story ending. If you're not sure what your genre is, take a guess and start there. Preparing your novel is about testing ideas and seeing how they fit together.

WHAT IS GENRE?

"Genre is a label that tells the reader/audience what

to expect. Genres simply manage audience
expectations." – Shawn Coyne, StoryGrid.com

There are many definitions of genre in fiction and
in storytelling in general. I like Shawn Coyne's defini-
tion from book, *Story Grid*, where he also has an
extensive discussion of how to analyze genre in his
material.

For example, readers of romance expect a Happily
Ever After or a Happily For Now. Mystery readers
expect a mystery at the beginning that is solved by a
sleuth and the perpetrator brought to justice. Thriller
readers expect a fast-paced ride where the main character runs for their life but finds a way to overcome in
the end, but maybe at great cost.

Orson Scott Card's book, *Characters and Viewpoint*,
gives another take on reader expectations: "Whenever
you tell a story, you make an implicit contract with the
reader. Within the first few paragraphs or pages, you
tell the reader implicitly what kind of story this is going
to be; the reader then knows what to expect and holds
the thread of that structure throughout the tale. . ."

You probably already know your expectations of
your genre. Hopefully, you read what you want to
write. If you don't, I highly recommend that you do.

Five Parts of an Elevator Pitch (or Story Summary)

With your genre and its ending in mind, think about
your story and brainstorm the following five parts.

Then you'll weave them together into a few sentences, forming a cohesive paragraph.

- Situation

Start with the situation, also called the initial action or premise. This is the beginning of the plot. Think about the action that starts your story and note that.

- Main Character

Next, describe your main character. If you have more than one main character, create an elevator pitch for each one.

- Primary Objective

The third element is the main character's primary objective. In your story, what does your main character initially want? What is their initial goal?

- Antagonist or Opponent

The fourth component is to clarify the main character's antagonist or opponent. You can also think of this as the central conflict. Who or what is keeping your main characters from getting what they want?

- Disaster That Could Happen

Lastly, take note of the disaster that could happen. What's the worst that could happen? This can be phrased as a question or a statement.

EXAMPLE #1

Here's a story's elevator pitch, broken down into its five components, then woven into a paragraph:

1. Abandoned on his relatives' doorstep as an infant, (Situation, Initial Action, or Premise)

2. Harry Potter (Main Character)

3. longs to understand where he came from and why he feels different. (Primary Objective)

4. He discovers that he is a wizard and that his parents were killed by Voldemort, a powerful and evil wizard, (Antagonist, Opponent, or Central Conflict)

5. who has been hunting for Harry, to kill him. (Disaster That Could Happen)

RECOGNIZE THIS? IT'S THE STORY SUMMARY of the first Harry Potter book, *Harry Potter and the Philosopher's Stone* by J. K. Rowling. The genre is fantasy and readers expect life and death stakes in a world unlike their own.

EXAMPLE #2

From *The Torah Codes* by Ezra Barany. See if you can spot the five components of an elevator pitch. The genre is thriller.

"A reclusive computer programmer, Nathan Yirmorshy, pounds out ones and zeros in the quiet of his home while his landlord secretly watches from behind a two-way mirror. When an intercepted note connects the landlord to a secret society, and a detective ends up dead, Nathan must abandon his home and everything familiar to him, open his heart to a tarot reader he has never met, and trust her with his life – just as the ancient scriptures have foretold."

Here is the above pitch segmented into parts:

1 and 2. A reclusive computer programmer, Nathan Yirmorshy

3. pounds out ones and zeros in the quiet of his home

4. while his landlord secretly watches from behind a two-way mirror. When an intercepted note connects the landlord to a secret society, and a detective ends up dead,

5. Nathan must abandon his home and everything familiar to him, open his heart to a tarot reader he has never met, and trust her with his life – just as the ancient scriptures have foretold.

EXAMPLE #3

From one of my novels, *A Labyrinth of Love and Roses*. Notice that since I have two main characters, I have one paragraph for each of them, and a third one-sentence paragraph for the fifth part of the elevator pitch.

"French MBA grad Lili Grenault needs to succeed at her last pitch meeting to fund her international green tech business. But her grandmother tells her to drop everything, find her one true love, and embrace her magical legacy by Beltane, in one week, or chaos and failure in her life will ensue.

"San Francisco investor Brett Barnaby wants to find his great-grandfather's gravesite in Amiens, France, one of the primary battle sites of World War I. Family legend says that purpose, greater mission, and perhaps even untold riches, will be unlocked when he finds that grave. But his search in Amiens brings up fear, anger, and dire warnings about some wild Green Man. He turns to local Lily Grenault for help.

"Can these two independent freethinkers work together to prevent chaos from triumphing and find love in time in the labyrinth of roses?"

Now broken out.

For Lili:

1 and 2. French MBA grad Lili Grenault

3. needs to succeed at her last pitch meeting to fund her international green tech business.

4. But her grandmother tells her to drop everything, find her one true love, and embrace her magical legacy by Beltane, in one week,

5. or chaos and failure in her life will ensue.

For Brett:

1 and 2. San Francisco investor Brett Barnaby

3. wants to find his great-grandfather's gravesite in Amiens, France, one of the primary battle sites of World War I. Family legend says that purpose, greater mission, and perhaps even untold riches, will be unlocked when he finds that grave.

4. But his search in Amiens brings up fear, anger, and dire warnings about some wild Green Man. He turns to local Lily Grenault for help.

5. Can these two independent freethinkers work together to prevent chaos from triumphing and find love in time in the labyrinth of roses?"

ACTION

Now it's your turn! Use the workbook to draft your elevator pitch using these five elements: Situation, Main Character, Primary Objective, Antagonist (Opponent, or Central Conflict), Disaster That Could Happen. Use this link to access the Bonus Workbook: http://bethb.net/bonusworkbook.

NEXT

In this next exercise, you'll draft your what-if pitch. Ezra, take it away.

FOUR

The What-If Pitch by Ezra Barany

*T*hanks, Beth.

You can write the what-if pitch before you write your first draft or after. I like to write it first-thing, even before I draft my story's elevator pitch. That's the way I roll.

Chances are you've asked yourself, "What if such-and-such happened? Wouldn't that make an amazing book?"

The benefits of crafting your story's what-if pitch is that you can use it to focus on while you write and to help you get re-energized anytime you forget what you're writing. Also, if you share your what-if pitch with others, they'll get a clear idea of the primary compelling conflict in your story. You may even turn people into eager fans, pestering you about when they can read your story.

How to Craft Your What-If Pitch

Think about the driving conflict in your story. Now draft a question under twenty words that conveys the main conflict of the story.

Check out these examples:

"WHAT IF PETER PAN GREW UP?"

–For the movie "Hook"

"WHAT IF DINOSAURS NEVER BECAME extinct?"

–For the movie "The Good Dinosaur"

"WHAT IF THE SAN ANDREAS FAULT split open?"

–For the movie "San Andreas"

SOMETIMES THE PITCH WORKS BETTER IF YOU start, "What would you do if...?"

For example, "What would you do if your beloved were on a hit list?" That one's for my thriller, *36 Righteous: A Serial Killer's Hit List*.

ACTION

Now it's your turn! Use the workbook to draft

your what-if pitch. http://bethb.net/bonusworkbook.
For maximum effect, keep it under twenty words.

NEXT

In this next exercise, Beth will guide you to draft
your story's synopsis with the help of a plug-
and-play tool.

FIVE

Your Story Synopsis

*L*et's open the story accordion a little bit more, accessing more about your story.

A synopsis is a short summary of your book. In the planning stages, it can help you think through the beginning, middle, and end of your story. The story synopsis tool I present here is a great way to think about the inner and outer changes for your two main characters, if you're writing romance. If you're not writing romance, this tool will still be able to help you brainstorm the inner and outer change for your main character.

Tip: If you do plan to pitch your story to a literary agent, editor, or publisher, you'll most likely need a synopsis. Once your novel is polished, you can come back to your draft of your synopsis and edit it.

This story synopsis tool, called a Plot Spinner, was designed by the award-winning romance author and writing teacher Patricia Simpson, and adapted from a workshop by Alicia Rasley, and used with kind permission.

As you craft your story synopsis with the exercise below, keep your genre in mind. This will give you a general ideal of your story's ending.

Your Story's Theme

Take a moment to think about the theme of your story. Notice what is top-of-mind for you. Is it a story about redemption or revenge or perhaps how love conquers all? Notice where your imagination goes. You'll need the story's theme for the Plot Spinner.

For some writers, it's hard to brainstorm the theme, since it's an abstract concept. But you may surprise yourself and discover that the theme you want to flesh out through your characters and their challenges is something that has been preoccupying you for some time, maybe even your entire life.

ACTION

Ready to dive into the Plot Spinner tool? Go here: http://www.patriciasimpson.com/PlotSpinner/snapsy nopsis.aspx.

Patricia walks you through each step with instructions.

Alternatively, you can use the outline below to draft your synopsis. For each step, Patricia Simpson shares examples.

. . .

ACTION

Number your page one through seven and pay attention to the subsections listed in individual letters "a-o." The out-of-order sequencing of the letters will be clear in the final step. You'll brainstorm your story's issue, theme, and then your main character's external struggle, internal struggle, and interaction. Use a maximum of one or two sentences for each item.

STORY SYNOPSIS IN 7 STEPS

1. ISSUE: What issue/theme do you want to explore in your story? Examples: Trust, Lust, Infidelity, Power, Control, Redemption, Love.

2. PREMISE: WHAT IS THE IDEA THAT YOU want to prove or disprove at the end of your story? Examples: You have to trust yourself before you can trust others. Once a cheater, always a cheater. Home is where the heart is. You can never go home again. There IS such a thing as love at first sight. To find a sense of home, sometimes you have to leave it.

ANSWER THE FOLLOWING, KEEPING THE ISSUE in mind that you chose in Step 1. Remember, use a maximum of one or two sentences for each item.

. . .

3.   HEROINE'S   INTERNAL   STRUGGLE
with issue:

d. At the beginning (Tatiana doesn't trust men.)

e. In the middle (Tatiana finds out Ren is using her
to break spell.)

f. At the end (Tatiana learns she has to trust
herself first before she can trust men.)

4. HEROINE'S EXTERNAL STRUGGLE BECAUSE
of issue:

a. At the beginning. (Divorce, caused by lack of
intimacy, has caused loss of house.)

b. In the middle (Tatiana is kidnapped when she
trusts villain.)

c. At the end (Tatiana must trust Ren to find trea-
sure to get house back.)

5. HERO'S INTERNAL STRUGGLE WITH ISSUE:

j. At the beginning (Women are to be revered or
bedded, not befriended.)

k. In the middle (Ren is confused about his
growing admiration & lust for Tatiana.)

L. At the end (Ren gets to know and trust a
woman for the first time in his life)

6. HERO'S EXTERNAL STRUGGLE BECAUSE
of issue:

g. At the beginning. (Ren has to woo a woman to

break the spell.)

h. In the middle (Ren realizes he will probably die before he seduces Tatiana.)

i. At the end (Ren chooses death to help Tatiana save her home.)

7. H&H (HERO AND HEROINE) INTERACTION:

m. At the beginning (Against his better judgment, Ren offers his services to Tatiana.)

n. In the middle (Just when she is softening toward him, she finds out why he is wooing her.)

o. At the end (Tatiana must trust Ren implicitly to save the house.)

TO PUT ALL YOUR NOTES TOGETHER, TAKE THE above sentences and arrange them into three paragraphs organized like this:

a, d, g, j, m

b, e, h, k, n

c, f, i, l, o

ACTION

Draft your synopsis using the Plot Spinner tool or the outline above. PRESTO! CHANGO! You should have the basic path of your story in fifteen sentences. String them together with modifying phrases so they make sense and are causally related.

· · ·

TO RECAP

In Week One, you were invited to brainstorm your story's

- Genre
- Elevator pitch
- What-if pitch
- Theme
- Synopsis

Use the workbook to jot down your notes or put your thoughts into a notebook, writing program, or Word document. You can get the workbook here: http://bethb.net/bonusworkbook.

NEXT

In Week Two, you'll brainstorm about your main characters—the lifeblood of every story.

Week Two: Get to Know Your Main Characters

SIX

Interview Your Characters

---

*I*n Week Two, we cover getting to know your main characters, so you can bring them to life when you write your novel.

I couldn't fit everything I know about developing characters and character arcs in this planning book, so if you'd like more in-depth work on developing your characters, I recommend checking out my home-study course, Craft Compelling Characters, and also the subject of a forthcoming book (Spring 2019.)

Week Two is my favorite week. I love thinking about my characters and answering all the brain-storming questions that I have for them. I use these questions for every novel I plan.

In this section, I expand on the Essential Tips for Characters from Chapter One, and I add questions, so you can uncover your character's:

- Strengths
- Hopes
- Fears
- Dreams
- Major turning point(s) in their past as it relates to the story (backstory)
- Important relationships
- Dress/clothing/significant objects
- Secrets
- Identity and core beliefs
- Emotional center

You can use the questions below to guide you and use the workbook to take notes:

http://bethb.net/bonusworkbook.

Interview Your Characters

Imagine one of your characters is sitting across the table from you, sipping a beverage, and looking at you. Keep your story in mind as you ask questions. Interview them and take notes. If you don't know your story at all yet, all the better. Let the interview unfold their story. Ask for specifics. Be detailed. Specifically, use sensory details, such as sight, sound, smell, touch, touch, and the internal body experiences.

If you have more than one main character in your story, answer these questions for each of them, including the antagonist or villain, and other important secondary characters.

Keep in mind your genre. This will give you a general idea of the kinds of characters that work best for the story you're writing. Also keep in mind how you think your character where they start from and how they will change.

For our characters to feel real, relatable, engaging, and compelling, we need to know them well. For some writers, myself included, I really get to know my characters when I'm writing the first draft and when I'm editing. But I don't skip this planning step. The answers you come up with will guide you with the rest of the planning, and when you're writing and editing.

Allow anywhere from one to fifteen minutes to answer each interview question for your character.

INTERVIEW QUESTIONS

1. WHAT WOULD YOU LIKE? WHAT GOALS DO YOU HAVE, externally and internally? What's your big vision for your life for the inner and outer goals?

An outer goal is tangible and external to your character. It's something anyone can see, touch, and hear.

An inner goal is a feeling experience, internal to your character, non-tangible and deeply personal.

2. WHY DO YOU WANT THESE THINGS? WHAT would happen if you didn't get them? In other words, what's at stake?

We're exploring your character's motivation. It's worth spending extra brainstorming time here and not stop with the first answer you get. Dig deeper and ask, "Once you have what you want, what will having that do for you?" Ask four or five times to see if you can get to the heart of the matter.

3. WHAT IS IN THE WAY OF YOU GETTING what you want? Other people? Circumstances? Fears? Concerns?

This question explores the conflict your character experiences. Conflict is an internal experience, including fears and contradictions. It is also an external experience, someone else wanting what the character has, or someone wanting what the character also wants. Either way it seems like only one person can have it.

4. WHAT ARE YOUR STRENGTHS? WHAT ARE you good at? What natural and learned skills do you have? What are your aptitudes? What things were you given, both literally and figuratively, that make your life good?

Explore your character's strengths. These could be things your character was born with as well as people, objects, education, and other experiences in their life.

5. WHAT ARE THE IMPORTANT RELATIONSHIPS

in your life and why? Describe who they are and what kind of relationship you have with each one?

Include both the good and the difficult relationships that feel key to the story and to your character.

6. WHAT KIND OF EDUCATION HAVE YOU received?

For your character's education, brainstorm what's relevant to your story, and include both the formal and the informal, the on-the-job training.

7. WHAT IS YOUR HOME LIKE? WHAT ARE YOUR living circumstances? How do you feel about where you live?

Describe the intimate details of their intimate environment. Be specific in your sensory details.

8. WHAT KIND OF TRANSPORTATION DO YOU use and how do you feel about it? What do you wish you could drive or take?

This may be self-explanatory, but don't skip it, in case their mode of transportation is relevant to your story and to your character's sense of self.

9. TELL ME ABOUT THE MOST TRYING EVENT or experience in your life. How does that relate to your goals?

Pick one event and describe the key sensory elements that deeply affected your main character. Search for the experience in their past, maybe far in their past, that shapes who they are today as it is relevant to your story, your story theme, and your story genre. What other key elements are important in their backstory that occurred to you that you want to jot down?

10. WHAT ARE YOUR MOST PRIZED possessions, things you can't live without? What do you carry with you everywhere and how: car, purse, backpack, back pocket, etc.? What meaning do these objects have to you?

One item can tell a lot about your character. Sketch out the object or find images for it. Be specific in the details. They matter to your character. Your job is to know what the object is and why it matters. This question is inspired by Tim O'Brien's book, *The Things They Carried.*

11. HOW WOULD YOU DESCRIBE YOUR appearance: height, weight, body type, etc.? How would someone else describe your appearance: love interest, villain, other important people?

How your character describes their appearance can tell a lot about their self-image. Knowing how other people view them allows you another insight into their relationships.

. . .

12. HOW WOULD SOMEONE ELSE, NOT YOU, describe your personality?

This question will give insight into your character's complexity. If you practice this question in the real world with your friends, you may hear a range of answers that show another sense of self.

13. WHAT HABIT, MANNERISM, OR TICKS DO you have?

If your character doesn't know their own ticks, interview someone close to them who would know. For the purposes of story planning, pick one or two specific actions that they do a lot.

14. HOW DO YOU LIKE TO DRESS? WHAT DO you normally wear? What's in your closet that you never wear? What do you wear for formal occasions? Informal occasions? Why do you make these choices? How do you feel towards clothing?

Perhaps a mundane topic, but how you clothe your characters can say a lot about their personality, their culture, and their work.

15. WHAT DO YOU DO FOR WORK? HOW DO YOU feel about it?

Inquiring about work can give insight into your

character's identity or conflicts and shed light on important relationships or areas of tension.

16. WHAT DO YOU REALLY HOPE FOR? WHAT do you yearn for? What do you dream about?

Ask each question to see if you trigger a different response, and don't settle for the clichéd or easy answer.

17. WHAT IS YOUR IMPOSSIBLE DREAM, THE one no one knows about?

Maybe you'll surprise yourself and your character with this answer.

18. IS THERE ANYTHING ELSE YOU HAVEN'T told me that you'd like to share?

Write down your authorly observations and anything at all that occurs to you to note about your character.

ACTION

Schedule time to get to know your characters. Dive into each question and see how far you get. You could do the above exercises in short chunks, ten to twenty minutes a day, or do them all in an afternoon or evening. Also, notice what you like about your characters and notice what surprises you or what you didn't like about them.

NEXT

We'll explore your character's sense of identity and core beliefs.

SEVEN

Uncover Your Characters' Core Beliefs And Identity And How They Change

A story is defined by change. Who is your character at the start of the story? This is what you explored with the questionnaire above. Who does she or he need to become to handle the rising challenges—the conflicts, both internal and external—of the story?

Before I start on the characters' core beliefs, I find it useful to first clarify the basic framework of my story, such key elements as theme and the goals, motivations, conflicts, and strengths for my main characters. (Week One)

I adapted this section on identity and beliefs from my training in NLP (neuro-linguistic programming or patterning) and brought them into my own fiction writing and into my courses and workshops teaching novelists. The discipline and practice of NLP developed to help people understand how we learn and change and to have the life we want. Since stories are about how our story's characters change in the face of their challenges—just like in real life—it felt natural to integrate my NLP training to help authors write more powerful stories.

BELIEFS

NLP Master Practitioner and author, Jon Low, says that beliefs are assumed associations that people make, consciously or unconsciously, in order to make sense of life. From our earliest age, we derive them from our experiences. Here are a few examples: Rich people are evil. Anything that has four legs and a lid is a chair and so can be sat on. Cars are for driving fast. Hard work pays off. Dogs are dangerous. Breakfast is the most important meal of the day.

Deep-rooted beliefs are almost unconscious and are the ones that really make a character a character. Think of a hero or heroine that shoulders the world and refuses help from his or her friends. They have a belief that, "There is something wrong with the world, and I'm the only one who can fix it."

We all have core beliefs. And there's usually one that predominates at any one given time and drives our actions. My NLP master teacher, Carl Buchheit, likens this core belief to a bowl full of grapes. All the grapes in the bowl are also core beliefs supported by the main one, the bowl.

Our core beliefs support us so that we can have a coherent sense of reality. Above all, our brain's job is to make sure everything makes sense. According to neuroscientist Anil Seth, "What we consciously see depends on the brain's best guess of what's out there." (TED Talk, 2017)

Our core beliefs also sometimes get in the way when one part of us starts to change but faces internal resistance. We often revise our core beliefs throughout our lives without noticing. Sometimes we do notice and may experience an internal fight—and sometimes an external one too when our lives "fall apart." It often isn't until we step into the new belief that our lives change.

IDENTITY

Low says identity are specifically beliefs about self. They are what form someone's personal image. For example, the lone main character might have an identity, "I am a loner." Or a detective character may have the identity, "I am a crusader."

ABOUT THE EXERCISE

In the identity and belief exercise, you'll brainstorm your main character's core beliefs. You'll also brainstorm the thoughts, words, feelings, and actions that stem from those core beliefs, both for the start of your story and for the end of your story.

You may be wondering how knowing your characters' starting and ending core beliefs is relevant and important to storytelling and to crafting a compelling character.

Here's why. Core beliefs define how we act, react, and how we make decisions. The same is true for our characters, especially if we want to create characters that feel real to our readers. Our core beliefs shape everything we do, including how we face conflict.

For example, in my romance novel, *A Labyrinth of Love and Roses*, Lili believes that work is the most important thing at the beginning of the story. This core belief colors everything she says, does, feels, and thinks. She speaks and thinks constantly about her work. Her actions? She works on her laptop all the time. Her feelings? She's upset about any distractions and is torn and frustrated by her grandmother's request to drop everything for a magical legacy. Her thoughts? About work, of course.

Now think about your story. At the start of your story, your character has a core belief about themselves that colors everything: their choices, their actions, and how they see the world. Their core belief also colors their relationship to themselves and to life itself.

Because of the story's rising conflicts, this core belief is challenged. They HAVE to change their belief about themselves to meet and overcome each of the emerging challenges, with a growing awareness of the shift. But not all at once. Their new core belief, and the accompanying sense of identity, is usually realized fully by the final climax of the story. (We'll get into story structure in the next section, Week Three.)

Let's dive deeper into your character's beliefs. The following exercise will help you experience a few of your core beliefs, and then help you brainstorm a few of your character's core beliefs.

DEEP DIVE EXERCISE FOR YOU AND YOUR CHARACTER

FOR YOURSELF

Do this Deep Dive exercise first for yourself, so you can apply the concept of core beliefs to your life and experience what I'm talking about. Then you'll repeat this exercise for your characters.

ACTION

Think of a time when you changed your belief about something. For the purposes of this exercise, pick something simple.

FOR EXAMPLE, I USED TO BELIEVE THAT peanut butter sandwiches every morning were the best breakfast for me. Now I don't believe that. Now I believe it's the worst breakfast for me.

My behavior changed; the story I tell myself (my thoughts) changed; how I feel about what I used to eat (my feelings), and about what I now eat—eggs and vegetable—changed (my action.)

ACTION

Now think about your writing. What do you think,

feel, and do in regard to your writing? How does this reflect your core belief? My NLP teacher says that if you want to know what you believe, look to your experience.

I'LL ILLUSTRATE WHAT I MEAN. IN MY CASE, I'm determined to be a prolific author. Therefore, I work on multiple projects (my action); I think about my projects (my thoughts), and I feel excited about them (my feelings). My core belief: "I am a fiction writer. I am creative. I am living my dream. I am worthy of living my dream."

In the past, before I made this decision to be consciously prolific, I felt I'd let myself down (my feelings), though I didn't know exactly why; I was working at my writing in fits and starts (my action); and I told myself I was too busy (my thoughts.) My core beliefs at the time: "I am waiting for permission... I am not ready... I am not good enough."

What shifted? What changed for me? I saw another author stand up in front of us at a writer's meeting and say, "Go for it! If you want success as an author, do the work. Now's the time. I'm prolific. I do the work. So can you."

I heard her say that and thought, "Why not? Why am I having this pity party? I'm as capable as she is, as savvy as she is. I don't feel as confident as she does—I don't have her experience of already having two dozen books in the marketplace—but I can start. If I don't start, will I feel as stuck and as disappointed in myself in a year?" This awareness got me into action.

Soon after that, I set up a writing schedule for myself. A few months later, I willingly jumped into a new project that resulted in my first romance novella being published in *Gargoyle: Three Enchanting Romance Novellas*. I would have never considered writing a romance novella if I hadn't already decided to take some risks and be open to writing more. Since then I've written and published four more romance novellas, a young adult fantasy trilogy, and am editing a four-book series in science fiction/mystery series.

Action

Now your turn: Notice your current core belief concerning your writing. Has it shifted in the recent past? If so, notice the thoughts, feelings, and actions that show the "before" and the "after." What is the core belief reflected in your experience before and after the change?

If you haven't experienced a shift, but would like to, define the experience you'd like to have. In your mind's eye, step into the future version of you, in six months or a year. If you're having problems visualizing this, put pieces of paper on the floor labeled "present" and "future" and step on the "future" to experience the differences. What is that version of you thinking, feeling, and doing? And what is the core belief that this future version of you has so they can have that experience?

Step back into your present experience as a writer, then again step into the future version of yourself.

Do this a few times, back and forth, and notice what the differences are, if any.

Now step one more time into the future version of you and have that version look back at the past version of you now, here.

What advice does this future version of you have to give you now?

Step back into your current self and receive that advice. Notice what that's like.

Get up and move around, allowing your body to integrate this information in just the ways you know how, and at the speed of integration that is just right for you.

Now let's look at your character's core beliefs.

Your Character

Explore your main characters' core belief at the start of the story and their thoughts, feelings, and actions around this belief.

For this exercise, think of a horizontal timeline. It can even help to draw a line.

ACTION

On one side, imagine your character at the start of the story.

- What do they know to be true about themselves and the world?
- How do they feel about that?
- What do they say to themselves and/or to other people about that?
- What actions (or non-actions) do they take in regard to that belief?

Now imagine your character at the end of story. They have faced all their conflicts and challenges and succeeded. It's okay if you don't know how yet. You'll figure that out later!

ACTION

Answer the questions again for your character at the end of the story.

- What do they know to be true about themselves and the world?
- How do they feel about that?
- What do they say to themselves and/or to others about that?
- What actions (or non-actions) do they take in regard to that belief?

Hopefully, there will be a huge difference from the beginning to the end. Notice if there is or isn't.

～

FOR FURTHER READING ABOUT THE HEART-centered transformational NLP I was trained in, check out the training center at http://www.nlpmarin.com. See also Carl Buchheit's book, *Transformational NLP: A New Psychology*, and Jon Low's book, *Your Brand of Distinction: Earn More Money, Stand Out from the Crowd, Touch the Hearts of Many*.

NEXT

On to exploring your character's secrets. Shh, it's a secret...

EIGHT

Your Characters' Secrets

*I*n this lesson, you'll be invited to brainstorm your character's secrets. Secrets and revealing secrets are what drive the reader to turn the page. As you brainstorm, think of your character in three moments: as they are at the beginning of the story, as the story progresses, and at the end of your story.

ACTION

1. Brainstorm the secrets your character knows but keeps from other characters in the story.
2. These secrets could be about things the character did in their past, could be their opinions or their feelings.

3. Brainstorm secrets that the main characters don't know, but a third character knows.

4. These secrets could be events, actions, things another character said or felt.

5. Brainstorm secrets the reader gets to know that the character does not.

6. When the reader knows these types of secrets, they feel smart, they worry for the main character, and they keep reading to find out more.

7. Brainstorm the secrets your character keeps from themselves.

8. What might be working below the surface, driving the character to action that even they don't know about?

NEXT

You'll brainstorm ways to help your readers emotionally connect with your characters with the empathy formula. Take it away, Ezra!

NINE

Draft Your Character's Emotional Core With The Empathy Formula

HOW TO GET YOUR READERS TO CONNECT WITH YOUR CHARACTERS BY EZRA BARANY

*T*hanks, Beth!

Have you ever read a story where it didn't matter much what happened to the main character because you didn't care about them? I've read a number of old fairy tales where I couldn't connect with the protagonist, so by the end of the story I thought the tale was interesting, but I wasn't moved. It's vital that your reader cares and worries about your characters, so they keep turning the pages. Here are ways to do just that.

This information comes straight from Karl Iglesias's presentation at Story Expo in Los Angeles on "The Emotional Core." (Sept. 2016) and shared with kind permission.

He presented it as a formula:

$$EC = Em \ (R + P^2 + H + A) + ES \ (WM)$$

Whoa. I know that looks a little complicated so let's break it down. Just so you know, in this case, everything in parentheses is not part of the formula but is meant instead to clarify what Em and ES are. The actual formula would be EC = Em + ES.

The Emotional Core (EC) equals Empathy (Em) (which is Recognition (R), plus Pity squared (P^2), plus Humanity (H), plus Admiration (A)) plus Emotional Stakes (ES), which is the character's Worthy Motivation (WM).

Let's dig a little deeper. The first part of the Emotional Core is made of Empathy. And Empathy is made up of four parts: Recognition, Pity, Humanity, and Admiration.

Emotional Core

1. Recognition:

We care about characters who are like us. Maybe your character is a mom who tells her son to place the silverware on the table. Once her son says he's finished and leaves, she goes around the table and repositions all the forks, knives, and spoons to their proper place setting. Maybe the reader can recognize their own drive to make sure everything is perfect. If the reader is a slob and doesn't care about perfection, it's likely they'll tell themselves, "I know someone who's exactly like that." By adding these "everyday" traits, your readers can recognize themselves in your story.

As an example of what wouldn't work: Imagine your adult protagonist eating candles. No one (hopefully) can recognize themselves, or anyone else, behaving in such a way.

2. PITY

We care about those we feel sorry for. This technique is great to create empathy for your villains and protagonists, alike. Also, it is so powerful that if you just use this technique and do nothing else to connect the readers to your characters, it's likely that you've done enough. That's why Pity is "squared."

Using pity in your story is a powerful way to build empathy. One way to create pity is to show undeserved mistreatment and injustice, especially if it's of a defenseless character. Show your character experiencing or observing undeserved misfortune, such as a tragedy or bad luck, or show a physical or mental handicap. Other ways to present pity are to show your characters as frustrated, humiliated, abandoned, betrayed, lonely, or neglected.

3. HUMANITY

We like characters who have humanistic traits. In other words, any time your characters care about anyone other than themselves, readers are drawn to who they are. This includes helping the less fortunate, relating to children or being liked by them, petting the dog or saving the cat or being loved by pets, showing humanity in private moments, risking their life for another human being, self-sacrifice or dying for a just cause, or any nurturing act such as kindness, caring, or generosity.

4. Admiration

We like characters who have qualities we admire. Be it power, charisma, courage (mental or physical), being passionate about something, being skilled at what they do, being witty and clever, being humorous, being active rather than passive, or being surrounded by others who adore them.

See if you can spot how Spike Jonze's award-winning IKEA commercial harnesses some of these empathy techniques:

https://www.youtube.com/watch?v=jU-cori2KU.

EMOTIONAL STAKES

The final part of the Emotional Core equation consists of the Emotional Stakes, a.k.a. the character's worthy motivation.

Ask yourself, what would happen if my character fails to accomplish their goal? Then what? Why would they keep going? Why would they keep fighting?

The failure is always death of some kind, be it physical, actual death, or emotional—it just feels like they're dying inside. Emotional death can feel like helplessness, hopelessness, or a numbness, depression. Anything less than death is an indicator that your character's stakes may not be high enough.

Common motivations for our characters are: survival, security, love, justice, humanism (doing something for another), and redemption.

What are your characters fighting for?

IN SUMMARY

If you incorporate some of the techniques for generating empathy and combine that with high stakes, your readers will love your characters, and you'll likely succeed in reaching that distinguished goal of touching your readers' hearts.

ACTION

For each of your main characters, write down the different aspects of touching your readers' emotional core.

Empathy (Em)

- Recognition (R)
- Pity squared (P^2) (The square means: if nothing else for Empathy, focus on this.)
- Humanity (H)
- Admiration (A)

Emotional Stakes (ES)

- The character's Worthy Motivation (WM).

For further reading: *Writing for Emotional Impact* by Karl Iglesias. More at:

http://www.karliglesias.com/portfolio/writing-for-emotional-impact/.

NEXT

Beth will walk you through the Character Relationship Map, a useful tool to brainstorm the relationships between your main character and the other characters in your story and how they change throughout your story.

TEN

The Character Relationship Map

*A*dapted from a TV writing tool, the Character Relationship Map is a useful way to brainstorm how your main characters and secondary characters relate to each other throughout your novel. When TV writers plan out their series, their seasons, and their episodes, they map out the character relationships to track them.

This tool is important and useful because stories are about how characters change as they pursue that all-important goal. Characters change because of external events, including the actions of other characters. They also change because of their internal experiences and decisions they make because of those external events.

ACTION

Write brief descriptions detailing how each of your characters feels about the others at the beginning, middle, and end of the story. You only need to list the main characters in your story—at a minimum, all the point-of-view characters; and at maximum, if you're ambitious, all the characters that you name.

Also, list how the characters feel about themselves. Check out the chart in the Bonus section to use and adapt as needed.

http://bethb.net/bonusworkbook.

Here's a screenshot of a blank Character Relationship Map:

This material is adapted from "Industry Insider TV Pilot Proposal" by Jesse Douma via The Writers Store.

NEXT

As we wrap up Week Two, you may still be wresting with what to write. Maybe you have doubts about what to focus on. If that's the case, read on to the next section to help you uncover what to write or to confirm that you're on the best path for you.

ELEVEN

Focusing on What to Write

*Y*ou may still be wrestling with what to write. Maybe you have lots of ideas or no ideas. Here's an exercise, created by Ezra, to help you uncover what you'd like to write.

Take it away, Ezra.

HOWDY, FOLKS!

Many authors are plotters and think an excellent way to start a book is to outline every scene first. Lots of other authors are pantsers, writing from the seat of their pants, who believe an excellent way to start a book is to put their characters in a situation and write what happens on the fly. The reality is, there are other items to consider first before either plotting or pantsing.

In this Venn diagram, you'll notice three sections.

Let's walk through each section and determine what your sweet spot is.

Your Sweet Spot

VENN DIAGRAM: How to Decide What To Write
What story is in the sweet spot for you?

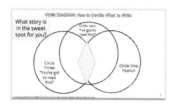

Circle One: What You Love to Write, Your Passion

This is the most important circle. You must write what you love because if you hate what you're writing or are bored by it, the reader will pick up on that and also be bored too. Your passion could be your favorite genre or subgenre, like thriller or romance. It could be a mood, like wry, comical, or dark. It could be a favorite type of character, like female athletes or spies.

ACTION

What genre, mood, or type of character do you love writing about?

. . .

CIRCLE TWO: "I'VE GOT TO READ THIS!"

When readers land on your book's sales page a vendor's site or your site, it's important to have something there that will capture their curiosity. You need a strong book title and book description to grab them.

Ask yourself, "What do I need to show the browsing readers that will lower their risk and raise their desire to buy?" They risk spending time and money on something they may not like.

Consider familiar topics or characters, like retellings of fairy tales. Do you see how having a book that's a spin on Snow White could intrigue the browsing reader more than a story about someone we haven't heard of before named Macy?

Also, offering insights can be compelling, like what it was like to be the first Parisian detective, a New York firefighter during 9/11, a slave in early America.

ACTION

How about your book? Figure out what it could have that will get browsing readers to say, "I've got to read this book!" Jot it down!

CIRCLE THREE: "YOU'VE GOT TO READ THIS!"

Addressing this circle could be the very task that makes or breaks your sales results. Since most book sales are based on word-of-mouth, the million-dollar question to ask yourself is, "What do I need to write to get people talking about my book?"

Good writing craft isn't enough in today's marketplace.

Overall, the answer to this question is, "Anything that will change the readers' lives."

I do that by incorporating controversial topics in my story. Maybe the reader will love that I'm preaching to their choir, maybe they'll despise my claims. Either way, they'll tell others about what they thought of the book.

If you can find a way to get the readers to change their beliefs or change the way they live their lives, they'll likely share with their friends how your book made a major impact on their lives.

ACTION

Brainstorm ideas for your story that will drive readers to say, "You've got to read this!"

BRING IT ALL TOGETHER

Once you have all your circles filled, see what's inside the sweet spot. What is something that will appeal to readers in the book's description (your elevator pitch), something that will change their lives, and something you are absolutely, positively excited to write about? If you've filled that sweet spot, then work on that book and get it published. I can't wait to read it.

Here are two examples.

Here's how Beth used this Venn diagram to decide to write *A Labyrinth of Love and Roses*. She did some of this analysis while she was planning and some after the book was done.

CIRCLE ONE: WHAT YOU LOVE TO WRITE, Your Passion: What she's passionate about: France, labyrinths, roses, Amiens, magic, romance stories, the Green Man myth.

CIRCLE TWO: "I'VE GOT TO READ THIS!": Romance readers love stories about fated lovers, redemption, and love stories about opposites attract. Lili wants to save the world and Brett seems intent on building wealth as his first priority.

CIRCLE THREE: "YOU'VE GOT TO READ THIS!": For Beth, this isn't something she decides ahead of writing, but something that emerges after she's written the first draft. She doesn't stress about this third element, if it isn't immediately apparent and discovers it by what readers say. For *A Labyrinth of Love and Roses*, she says the two strongest "You've Got to Read This!" components are magic and destiny.

HERE'S HOW I USED THIS VENN DIAGRAM TO decide to write *The Torah Codes*, the first book in the series by the same name.

. . .

CIRCLE ONE: WHAT YOU LOVE TO WRITE, Your Passion: I love thrillers, codes, and twists!

CIRCLE TWO: "I'VE GOT TO READ THIS!": When I published this Jewish version of *The Da Vinci Code*, that book was still popular. So people who loved *The Da Vinci Code* also wanted to read my book.

CIRCLE THREE: "YOU'VE GOT TO READ THIS!": In The Torah Codes, I included scientific proof of God's existence. My readers would probably not want to go around saying, "Guess what? Turns out God's real. Ain't that a pickle snapper! Instead, they'd probably rather say, "You've got to read this!"

BACK TO BETH!

SUMMARY

Thanks, Ezra! In Week Two, you got to know your main characters and were invited to do these exercises:

- Interview Your Characters
- Core Beliefs and Identity
- Your Characters' Secrets
- Draft Your Character's Emotional Core With The Empathy Formula

- Character Map

You we're also invited to uncover what to write or to confirm that you're on the best path for you in the "Focusing on What to Write" section.

NEXT

We'll dive into Week Three to help you open up your story's accordion and help you shape the major structure of your story.

Week Three: Story Plot Points & World Building

TWELVE

Uncover Your Character's Worst Fears to Discover Your Story Conflicts

*I*n Week Three, we help you brainstorm these three elements: your character's fears to develop your story's important events, world building, your story's basic and essential building blocks. There's also a lesson on how to ask good questions, in case you're stuck. Sometimes we can get unstuck by asking our muse different questions.

Just a reminder about the creative brainstorming process: Things don't have to be perfect for you to be able to move forward with your story. Keep going! The magic of creating our stories happens in the doing. If you need to take a break to replenish the muse, definitely do that. And then come back to the brainstorming.

First up, I invite you into a new way to discover the problems, conflicts, and challenges your character may face in your story.

Uncover Your Character's Worst Fears to Discover Your
Story Conflicts

I'm a pantser. That means I like to write my stories by the seat of my pants. The problem was, when I started writing novels, the inspiration for my story and the love of my characters wasn't enough. I needed a way to figure out the story, but all the standard plot tools didn't work for me very well. I was stuck on how to create a compelling story that would keep me and my readers riveted to the page and caring about what happened to my dear characters. I didn't really understand how to create conflict. I felt like I would only stumble onto conflict by accident.

One day at a writing workshop, the teacher had us brainstorm our character's worst fears, then think of the worst thing after that, and even further, think of the even worse fear after that.

I did this exercise and shuddered in fear at all the horrible things I dreamed up for my character. And then I experienced an Aha!

The Aha wasn't that I scared myself with my imagination, even though that's what happened.

My Aha was that I could use what I was already good at—knowing my characters well—to craft the conflict of my story.

So, that's what I do now. After getting to know my characters well, as we shared in Week Two, I spend time uncovering their worst fears. Next, I turn these fears into bad things that happen to my character, so that my story's conflict is rooted firmly in my character.

Here's how you can do the same...

ACTION: Exercise: "List of 20"

Think about all you've discovered about your main character and what you know about your genre. Then do the following exercise.

On a piece of paper or on your computer writing program or in dictation, create a numbered list from 1 to 20. Then set the timer for 10 or 20 minutes.

Now brainstorm your character's worst fears. Keep moving your hand across the page to uncover more worse possibilities. And keep making things worse for your dear, sweet characters.

If you're stuck, ask: What is she really afraid of? What does he not want to see or acknowledge? It's okay if you write phrases, questions, or single words, or whatever else occurs to you. There are no wrong notes. It's a brainstorming exercise!

Keep in mind that this is just a list of ideas, and you may or may not use all of these. What's important is to write down as many fears as you can. If you find yourself drafting other ideas, just go with it. There are no mistakes, only information for your creative mind.

You may be surprised at what you discover.

Ding!

Time's up. Pencils down!

Take a break from your work if you need to. Then review your list.

- Organize your character's fears from bad to worse.
- Circle the fears that are external. If there aren't any, add some.
- Underline the fears that are internal. If there aren't any, add some.
- Make notes on the scenes you could write from each of these fears.
- Place these scenes in an order that makes sense for you and your story.
- Notice what surprised you and what gave you chills of excitement and/or fear. How can you use those strong emotions in your portrayal of your character's fear?

EXAMPLE

Here's my List of 20 from the third book in my Henrietta The Dragon Slayer series, *Henrietta and the Battle of the Horse Mesa*. I needed to give Henrietta lots to deal with.

1. What if she gets lost in the new land, Land of the Horse?
2. Franc, her bodyguard and maybe boyfriend, gets abducted.
3. She's afraid of facing the boy's mother.
4. The Horse people she's meeting have a "no strangers" policy in their land; she's nervous about meeting them; even if she's returning

the leader's son. What if they attack? What if the rumors are true about how they treat strangers? (Death by fire ants.)

5. She's not sure how her new powers will evolve and are evolving. Magic is as confusing as ever.

6. She knows she hasn't dealt with the bad guy fully; when will he show up?

7. Is she putting the Horse people in danger by going to their lands while the bad guy is still after her?

8. How will she handle the king's request to lead the army, especially when she doesn't want to?

9. She's afraid to know the answer to this question: Who are you if you strip away your sword, your fighting abilities, and your knowledge of the land?

10. As she gets further and further into the dry landscape of the Land of the Horse, she feels stranger and stranger, and feels like she's losing connection to the land. That freaks her out.

11. She feels unmoored, resource-less, without her ability to read the signs via the landscape and the birds. Panic!

12. She's torn between tracking down leads of bad guy skirmishes and finding Franc. She's faced with what feels like an impossible choice.

13. Antoine, the boy, still sometimes clings to

her as if she's his mother, even though his mother is right there. She can't be a mother. Too much to lose. And in what way will his mother retaliate?

14. She sees Paulette in a vision. What Paulette is doing — some kind of magic in a strange setting — confuses and scares her because it seems that Paulette has gotten more powerful. Does that mean that Paulette has gone from a friend to an enemy?

15. The leader of the Land of the Horse intimidates her; Henrietta feels like a beginner again and hates that.

16. In a ceremony, Henrietta has a vision that she doesn't understand. She hates not knowing.

17. She feels cut off from all she knows but senses the coming war (and sees it again in a vision), and really wishes she could ignore that, but knows she can't. She is not looking forward to the coming war, at all.

18. She has to work with the leader of the Land of the Horse to find Franc. It's not an easy adjustment for her. What makes it hard, besides the language barrier is the leader's method of leading. Henrietta is confused and overwhelmed by it. And she feels the fear of potentially losing Franc and hates how her heart and gut are twisted in fear; she's making stupid decisions because of this all-pervasive

sense of losing Franc. She feels like she's losing her mind.

19. When she gets word that Franc has been found at the Cliff of Five Points, she knows it's a trap. His life is riding on her successful rescue of him, all the while having to manage her unruly magic, her intense fear of losing Franc, and the need to lead several armies. How did she ever get to this knotty situation?

20. On the battlefield, all who she holds dear are there: Jaxter, Paulette, Franc, Antoine, Antoine's mother, and the good people of the Land of the Horse, and her compatriots in the Kingdom of Bleuve's army. And she has to make the right decisions to mitigate the casualties and crush the master villain — the most powerful sorcerer the Five Kingdoms have ever seen. No easy task. So much responsibility for her. Can she pull it off?

MY AHAS: THIS WAS MY ACTUAL BRAINSTORM list for this book, now published. I didn't use all of these ideas, but they definitely inspired me in the first drafting process. When I reviewed my list before sharing it with my students for the first time, I got chills and tears as I added details. I was on the right track and couldn't wait to craft more Lists of 20 for my other main characters: Franc, Paulette, Antoine and his mother, Jaxter, and definitely the villain. This list helped me get more and more excited about this story, which would probably shape up to be my longest novel yet. And it was! At over 100,000 words —400 pages—*Henrietta and the Battle of the Horse Mesa* is indeed a big book, and a fitting final installment to the trilogy.

~

NEXT

In the next lesson, you'll be asked to brainstorm important details of your story world, so that your story can be more fully realized.

THIRTEEN

World Building: Questions to Brainstorm

*T*hough written with science fiction and fantasy writers in mind, world building applies to all writers. Here's why: You can use the details of your world to reveal character, ratchet up the tension, and move the story forward. But first you need to know your story world. You can discover it as you go—many writers do this, myself included—and, you can also prime your imagination by brainstorming as much as you can ahead of time. As if you're making a movie, you're the set designer, sound engineer, costumer, and props master (and more!) for your world.

I specifically encourage you to build your story world from the perspective of your main characters. It is their story after all, and the reader wants to experience the story world through their heart, mind, and body.

Overwhelmed with World Building? Let's Break it Down

Do you feel overwhelmed when you sit down to write about your fantasy or science fiction world? I know I have, so I've found some entry points into world building.

The strongest entry point for me is my characters. I interview my main characters—the point of view characters and the named secondary characters—to learn about my fantasy world.

If my main character can't tell me what I need to know, I interview secondary characters. In fact, I interview all my characters, even the minor ones, to learn about my world. In fact, I've invented an "off screen" character to learn more about my story world. That's sometimes how characters get "on screen."

You may not know all the parts of your world, nor will all parts of your world end up in your book. I most often start with the facts and lore that just flows from my subconscious and research the rest.

You may do it the other way around. You may be curious about something, start researching it, and then get inspired. I've done that too.

For example, my young adult fantasy heroine, Henrietta, was trained to be a blacksmith and sword smith. Why? Because I'm interested in those things. I researched by visiting a black smith and by reading about medieval sword construction and use. That was fun!

For my science fiction murder mystery series, I often started by researching the current and upcoming technology, and then got inspired on how to use it in my story.

Research is Fun...

Note: If the research isn't fun, STOP. The first person you get to please is yourself, so research only the things that are fun. What is joy-producing for you is also a clue that you're on the right path with your research and your story.

While I loved researching 1850s Paris and asking question about how Paris was built to become the marvel it is today, it was tortuous trying to write a novel set in that period. However, if I think of a time travel story that uses that period, then I'm on fire. Notice what sets you on fire and use that as background, back story, and setting. Your readers will sense your passion and be engaged.

How to Start Your World Building

The process of world building is a personal one, so each of you will discover or has discovered your own method of creating your story world. As I shared, I start with my main character, her GMC (Goal, Motivation, Conflict), her backstory and history, then start developing the world with that material. From there, other characters and their stories start fleshing out the world. Then I look at plot, and as I develop that, I come up with more questions and answers about the world. As I write and edit my book, I answer new questions that arise about the story world. Later, when my critique partners ask me questions about my story world, I flesh out those too. All this is to say that I don't sit down with the list below and fill in the blanks. I tried that once, and it didn't work for me. But it may work for you.

Try one way, and if that doesn't work, try another. You'll eventually find the way that works for you.

A Note on Fantasy versus Science Fiction and Making Up Stuff

Though we can blur the lines between the fantasy and science fiction, I want to draw a distinction on how we make up stuff for each genre. From what I understand and have read, you can make up everything when you write fantasy. You can do this as long as everything holds together logically and has meaning for your characters. If the world you're building feels random and that's not your intent, then you need to spend time figuring out the Why and How of things.

If you want to make up words, that's cool, as long as you and your reader don't get confused.

For science fiction, the world is usually based in some scientific possibility. We aren't traveling the stars yet, but one day we could be. We don't time travel (yet!), but according to physics there isn't any reason why one day we couldn't.

Questions to Ask While World Building

Here are some of the things I ask my characters about. Use these categories to guide you and add more categories as needed. Only answer what's relevant or useful to your story world and leave the rest. Use the bonus workbook handout to fill out the details of your world: http://bethb.net/bonusworkbook.

- **Language** — Does your world have different languages? How did they evolve?

- **Origin Tales** — How did the world come to be? How do people explain the world's origins?

- **Folklore** – What is your favorite childhood folktale or fairytale? What are the popular tales of the day? How do you feel about those?

- **Family Tree** – What do you know about your family tree? What do you wish you knew?

- **Jobs/Professions** — What kind of jobs do people have? Do men and women divide work, share it? What kind of training do your characters receive, if any? How are they trained and by whom?

- **Gender Roles** – What are people's attitudes about gender roles? What are the typical roles and why?

- **Clothing/Costumes** — How do people dress? What do your friends and colleagues wear and why? Where does fabric come from? Who makes it?

- **Weather** – What kind of seasons does your location have? How do you feel about that?

- **Flora & Fauna** – What are some of the important or relevant animals and plants where you are?

- **Food** — How is food planted, harvested, hunted, gathered? What do people eat and when? How is it cooked? Who cooks? What's poisonous?

- **Geography** – What are the main geographical regions of your land?

- **Annual Rituals** — What rituals are important to your world and why? How do you celebrate weddings, funerals, birthdays, puberty, other?

- **Technology** – What kind of technology

exists? How is it powered? Who creates it? What training do they need?

- **Animals** – Are there any special or magical animals in your world? What kind of pets do people have? What special relationship do you or others have with special animals?

- **Religion/Spirituality** – What are your religious or spiritual beliefs? What is your area's main belief system? How could people's religious or spiritual beliefs create conflict and why?

- **Magic** – What are the rules and boundaries around magic?

- **Politics/Power** – Who is in power and why? How is power transferred to the next generation? What can people do or not do to get close to powerful people?

A Special Note About Time Travel

If you're writing time travel, then you need to figure how and why it works.

If your story is fantasy-based, the time travel rules can be different and based in magic.

If you're writing science fiction, then your audience will expect you've figured out ways around the paradoxes that our modern readers will know (like the causal loop) and explain them within the logic of your story world.

HAVE FUN!

Have fun with your world building.

Whether you start with your characters to discover the story world, or you start with the world and add your characters, world building can be a wonderful process of discovery to create compelling and engaging worlds for our readers.

NEXT

Now that you've explored your character's fears, and you know your story world better, it's time to shape the broad outlines of your story using basic and essential building blocks of every story: the beginning, middle, and the twist.

FOURTEEN

Your Story's Structure

"Every story ever can be broken down into three parts. The beginning. The middle. And the twist." – R. L. Stine in the Goosebumps movie (2015)

*E*very story is a journey of some kind, a journey of change. And every story has a beginning, middle, and end. In this lesson, I'll explore this basic structure of every story. Yet, these three components will vary according to the kind of story you're writing. To keep things simple, think about your genre as it relates to the marketplace.

Remember, genre is about reader expectations, which changes with time and tastes. Each of these genres has typical beginnings, middles, and ends, moments the reader expects to see in that type of story. Shawn Coyne of StoryGrid.com calls these Obligatory Scenes: "Beginning Hook," "Middle Build," and "Ending Payoff." Genres also have typical kinds of characters and typical story elements or story conventions.

As you read through this list, think about how these types of stories typically begin.

- Romance
- Mystery
- Suspense
- Thriller
- Adventure
- Women's fiction

I'll explain these obligatory scenes in the context of the romance, thriller, and mystery genre.

ROMANCE

The romance genre has many sub-genres, each with their own reader expectations, but for the purposes of this book, I will keep my example general.

At the beginning of a romance, no matter the sub-genre, readers expect the lovers to meet. The Beginning Hook could be two potential lovers getting tangled at the dog park or finding themselves lost together or getting set up by well-meaning friends. The possibilities are endless, only limited by your imagination. Even if the two lovers are meeting for the first time, the reader needs to know and expects to see that they could become a couple. Or, if they once knew each other, when the lovers meet again after a long break, the reader needs to see the attraction and the potential for reunification, even if the lovers can't see it or don't believe it.

In romance's Middle Build, the reader needs to see and experience all the complications that keep the lovers apart. This is often competing agendas—they each want something different or they each want what the other has, and believe only one can win; or they're busy with their separate goals and don't yet see the value of being together, even though circumstances keep throwing them together; or maybe they need each other to succeed in their goals but deny or fight that.

In romance, for the Ending Payoff, we give the reader what she has been eagerly waiting for: the final climax and the Happily Ever After (or Happily for Now). The specifics of this will depend on your story and may bookend the opening scene or echo another moment within the story.

The kinds of characters we expect to see in a romance include the lovers, perhaps a mentor, a best friend, and an ex or competitor.

The kinds of story elements or story conventions readers expect to see in romance include the "First Kiss," a "Declaration of Love," the reasons to stay apart, and the "I love you" moment. Readers also like to see a new start/new beginning at the end, often in the form of an Epilogue, a peek at the new normal the lovers now experience.

THRILLER

Let's look at the Thriller genre. The Beginning Hook often entails the hero discovering that they are being hunted, like in *Bourne Identity*.

The Middle Build includes the hero, and maybe their companions, being chased.

The Ending Payoff is often a confrontation between the hero and the villain, with the story ending in either justice, injustice, or irony (justice isn't served in the way the reader expects.) The hero decides to stop running and confront those chasing them.

The kind of characters readers expect to see in thrillers include the hero who is often the victim in much of the story, innocent victims, the villain (one or many), the mentor, the buddy, the kind strangers, and the surprising ally.

Typical Story Elements include the hero's sacrifices, red herrings, time locks, and the speech in praise of the villain. Shawn Coyne goes into great depth about the thriller genre, using *The Silence of the Lambs* by Thomas Harris as his example throughout his book, *Story Grid: What Great Editors Know*. All the same information is on his website, www.storygrid.com.

A time lock is a deadline that forces the main character's hand to act. For example, the bomb must be diffused in three minutes. The hero must race to catch a plane. The princess will turn into a wench at the stroke of midnight.

A red herring is "something that misleads or distracts from a relevant or important issue. It may be either a logical fallacy or a literary device that leads readers or audiences towards a false conclusion. A red herring might be intentionally used, such as in mystery fiction..." (Wikipedia: https://en.wikipedia.org/wiki/Red_herring)

MYSTERY

Mystery, like romance, has many subgenres. For the purpose of this book, I'll paint the broadest strokes. But think of your subgenre as you brainstorm the obligatory scenes, typical characters and story conventions.

The Beginning Hook of a mystery is usually the discovery of a dead body or a theft. Sometimes the main character discovers the dead body, sometimes it's a minor character. Sometimes a crime is brought to the main character's attention by a client.

In the Middle Build, the main character hunts for clues and needs to parse out what's a valid clue and what's not.

At the Ending Payoff, the main character often confronts the villain and uncovers the truth, brings the criminal to justice, or faces an injustice or irony.

Typical characters include an investigator, like a detective, or eager amateur, prime suspects, innocent victims, a side kick like a "Watson-type," and villain.

Typical story elements include collection of evidence, red herrings, reluctant witnesses, inscrutable evidence, inductive and deductive reasoning, hunches, and a deadline (a time lock).

THE TWIST

A story twist is something unexpected. While readers expect the Beginning Hook, Middle Build, and Ending Payoff in your story with certain types characters and story elements, they also want to be surprised. It's our jobs as writers to make these elements surprising to our readers. How do you do that?

To create twists in your story, start with what's expected, then add in something the reader doesn't expect. You can use humor, opposites, the unusual or bizarre (something far outside the norm), or something embarrassing or shocking.

The twist is also often the part that readers and movie goers don't reveal to others. They might just say, "You have to see this movie!" Or, "You have to read this book." Like with the movie, *The Sixth Sense*. Or the book, *The Kite Runner* by Khaled Hosseini. And many more.

To help you come up with twists, there are more brainstorming tools in the workbook. Sign up for that here: http://bethb.net/bonusworkbook.

ACTION

Use the workbook to brainstorm these essentials for your genre: Beginning Hook, Middle Build, Ending Payoff, Characters, and Story Elements.

FOR FURTHER READING

For more information about story structure discussed in this section, check out "The Five Commandments of Storytelling" on Shawn Coyne's site: http://www.storygrid.com/466/.

NEXT

Sometimes writers get stuck in the brainstorming process and don't know what to do. It can be helpful to fall back on some tried-and-true journalism tools of asking basic questions. I'll call it the Question Toolkit. You can use it to ask good questions, which can help you unlock your story and get back to brainstorming and eventually writing your novel.

FIFTEEN

The Question Toolbox

Quis, quid, cur, quomodo, ubi, quando, quibus auxiliis. (Who, what, why, how, where, when, with what)

— Boethius (Early 6th century Roman Philosopher)[1]

*J*f you find that you are stuck in your story planning and brainstorming, instead of powering through, pause and ask questions. Our brains are wired to construct a coherent reality and to search for answers. All you need to do is trust the process. Ask questions of your subconscious and let your mind find the answer when you are doing something else, like taking a shower, walking the dog, or doing the dishes. Use one or more of these question openers to open up your creativity to discover what's next in your story, uncover an answer, or shake you loose from writer's block or the creative doldrums.

THE 5 Ws + HOW

Use these interrogative words to unlock the stuck areas:

- What
- Why
- Who
- When
- Where
- How

HERE ARE SOME EXAMPLES OF QUESTIONS YOU can ask of your characters:

- What is happening to my main character here? What do I want to have happen?
- Why would my character take this action at this time?
- Who are the most important characters in this part of the story?
- When does story really begin?
- How can I add more tension to this story?

My question to you: What questions can you ask to help you unlock your story?

. . .

HERE ARE MORE EXAMPLES FOR YOU TO ASK of your story and of your characters:

- What next?
- What's the worst thing that can happen next to my main character/point of view character?
- What else could happen?

STEP BACK AND ASK OVERALL STORY questions like these:

- Why would anyone care about this story?
- Why would anyone care about my character's story?
- How do I make this story memorable? What do I need to write to get my readers to tell their friends about this book?

TO RECAP

In Week Three, we helped you get to know the shape of your story better—the beginning, middle, and end—and helped you explore your story's world. You were also invited to uncover your main character's big fears to find the major conflicts in your story.

～

NEXT

In the final section of the book, you'll be invited to bring all of what you know about your characters and story into a coherent scene-by-scene outline. We'll help you do that whether you're a plotter who needs to know every detail before you write, or an organic writer, who wants a lot of space to discover the story as you write, but also want a roadmap so you don't get too lost along the way.

---

1. https://en.wikipedia.org/wiki/Five_Ws

Week Four: Scene-By-Scene Outline And Plotting

SIXTEEN

High-Concept Pitch

*I*n Week Four, we guide you through the final preparation step of building your story scene-by-scene. We help you create an organic outline from all the notes and thinking that have gone before and also provide tips on a more linear approach to plotting your story. Once you have completed this exercise, and all the ones before, you'll have a good sense of your entire story, and can sit down to write your novel with excitement and confidence.

Specifically, the lessons in this section are: a high-concept pitch, the problem-solution tool, scene structure, scene storyboarding, and a scene-by-scene outline.

Take it away, Ezra!

High-Concept Pitch by Ezra Barany

Thanks, Beth!

The purpose of this exercise is to help you get the 30,000-foot view of your story and thereby gain a new perspective. I use this tool with every book because it helps me understand the theme of my story.

No one cares what your story is about, though they think they do. They only care about the experience your novel will give them. A blurb or elevator pitch summarizing the story can convey the experience, but a high-concept pitch usually does a quicker job, since it's no more than five words.

With just a few words, convey the kind of book your story is by blending together two other famous stories or by defining a unique twist to a famous story. Mix and match and cross genres.

For example, a movie about an ancient species of shark terrorizing today's beaches could be pitched as "Jurassic Park meets Jaws." Shortened it's "Jurassic shark." This pitch immediately conveys the experience by conjuring familiar experiences we've had from other famous media (books, movies, music, etc.) A great marketing tool, the high-concept pitch is easy for your friends and family to repeat to their friends and family and accurately pass on the excitement of the book.

When I was initially marketing my first novel, *The*

Torah Codes, I'd say that it was "a Jewish version of *The Da Vinci Code*." Right away people knew to expect a thriller with clandestine religious overtones.

The common format for the high-concept pitch is "[famous movie or book] meets [other famous movie or book.]"

OTHER EXAMPLES:

- Lara Croft meets Lord of the Rings (for Beth's *Henrietta The Dragon Slayer* series)
- CSI in space (for Beth's upcoming *Janey McCallister Space Station* mystery series)
- Snakes on a Plane (a high-concept and a movie)
- The Wild West in Space
- Abraham Lincoln meets Vampires
- Starman meets Green Acres (For a forthcoming novel by one of our students; used by kind permission)
- A Quentin Tarantino western set in West Africa (from a forthcoming graphic novel by one of our students)
- When Harry Met Sally meets Portlandia, for the millennial generation
- Star Wars meets Pretty Woman (for the debut novel *An Alien Exchange* by one of our students, Keri Kruspe; used by kind permission)

As a brainstorming tool, focus on capturing the essence and don't worry about it being right at this point. You can always come back to edit this later.

ACTION

What is your high-concept pitch? Play with a few and then test them out on your friends. Use the handout in the Bonus Workbook material: http://bethb.net/bonusworkbook.

RESOURCES FOR FURTHER STUDY: *Got High Concept: The Key to Dynamic Fiction that Sells!* by Lori Wilde; "How to Write a High Concept Pitch" https://www.fuseliterary.com/2016/06/15/how-to-write-a-high-concept-pitch/

NEXT

Beth will share with you the problem-solution tool to help you set up your plot in a linear, step-by-step way.

SEVENTEEN

Design Your Plot with the Problem-Solution Tool

*T*hanks, Ezra!

Now that you have brainstormed your characters and your story world using the first three sections of this book, it's time to set up the plot in a linear, step-by-step way.

Years ago, when I was working on my first novel, I didn't know where to begin. Luckily, I stumbled on the book, *The Weekend Novelist* by Robert J. Ray, and used it as a guide to write every weekend to get going. One of the tools I really liked was the "problem-solution" tool, helping me design my story plot in a quick way. Since plot was confusing to me, this tool helped me get a handle on it. This tool helped me drill down to the scene level and start imagining what is actually happening in the story and how things resolve—but still get worse—until the end of your story.

Here's how it works. Ask yourself these questions (more questions!):

1. What's the starting problem of your story?
2. What's the solution to this immediate problem?
3. What problem is caused by this solution?
4. Create a new solution,
5. Which creates a new problem.
6. This leads to a new solution,
7. new problem...
8. Etc. until you get to your story resolution.

Your notes may look something like this...

HERE'S AN EXAMPLE BRAINSTORM FROM ONE section of my novel, *Henrietta and the Battle of the Horse Mesa*.

PROBLEM: HENRIETTA HAS TO CROSS THE mountains in the middle of winter with a small child who seems to have two identities and who she can't understand most of the time, and who calls her Mommy.

- Solution: Luckily, she has Franc with her to help her manage the boy, so she can focus on navigating the tricky mountain passes she knows well.

PROBLEM: WHILE THEY REACH THE PEAK without incident, the eastern side of the mountain is a steep and unfamiliar climb down.

- Solution: Antoine takes charge in his strange way and guides them to the bottom, all the while chattering away in his native tongue. They are, after all, walking back into his land.

PROBLEM: THEY'RE WALKING INTO A LAND NO foreigner is supposed to go. All who have ventured here have never returned. The rumor is that they were killed.

- Solution: Henrietta hopes their chances for survival are better since they are returning a child of the Land of the Horse.

ACTION

Design your plot using the problem-solution tool and find your way into and through your story. Use the workbook to draft your notes:

http://bethb.net/bonusworkbook.

~

NEXT

We dive into what are the five essential elements of a scene, so you can start writing with a clear picture in your mind.

EIGHTEEN

Five Essential Stages Of A Scene (And Of Story!)

"As Shawn Coyne always says, stories are about change. There has to be a change in every unit from the global story down to the micro beat. This applies to writing scenes as well." — Rebecca Monterusso

These five essential stages of a scene come from Shawn Coyne's *Story Grid*. When you know what your scene is about, then you need to know how to craft a scene in a way your readers can relate to. Each of the five elements can also be applied to looking at your story as a whole.

Every scene starts with an Inciting Incident. Coyne says it's "...the big event that kicks off your story" (or Scene.)

Next, your scene needs a Progressive Complication. The story, as a whole, needs many of these "...escalating degrees of conflict that face the protagonist."

Also called a Turning Point, this moment occurs by your character action—something they do or something they realize, a revelation.

Next comes the Crisis moment. This moment is "...a question that offers a choice between two options." The character faces either the Best Bad choice or has to choose between two great things but can only have one.

Finally comes the Climax, "...the moment when a character acts on his crisis choice...the truth of character...the active answer to the question raised in the crisis..."

Lastly, the scene ends with the Resolution. "The resolution...is crucial for the reader or viewer to fully metabolize the story."

LET'S BREAK IT DOWN WITH AN EXAMPLE I drafted for a possible opening scene for my next romance novel about Hank and Isabelle, tentatively called *The Alchemy of Love*.

INCITING INCIDENT: Hank, a night security guard at a specialized university archaeology research center, hears a strange sound in the lab and goes to investigate.

PROGRESSIVE COMPLICATION: He sees a stranger approaching one of the researchers and calls after him. The stranger runs, and Hank runs after him through the building exit into the back alley behind the building.

CRISIS: Should he follow the stranger farther and leave the researcher alone or stay in the lab and have no further clues for the police?

CLIMAX: He chooses not to follow the stranger but instead calls the police. His first duty is to the lab, its artifacts, and researchers.

RESOLUTION: He feels satisfied that he did his job well and that the researcher, Isabelle, feels safe.

My next scene starts with Isabelle not feeling safe after the break-in, even though the capable and good-looking night guard did his job. That's the inciting incident of the next scene.

RECAP

Use these five essential elements to keep the momentum of your scene going and to make sure the stakes are raised with each new scene.

ACTION

Your turn: Draft the five essential elements of your scenes, using the workbook or your own document. The bonus workbook can be accessed here: http://bethb.net/bonusworkbook.

FOR FURTHER READING, CHECK OUT "THE Five Commandments of Storytelling:"

http://www.storygrid.com/466/.

NEXT

We explore storyboarding or setting up your scene, a great way to visualize the details of your scene.

NINETEEN

Scene Setup: Storyboarding

*W*hat makes up a scene? When I was first starting out as a novelist, this was a conundrum to me. It's a mystery to many of the novelists I've worked with too.

A scene is action that takes place in one place and time.

Think of your story as a stage play. Each time you have to change the set to show a new location, you're starting a new scene. To get started, use this scene setup tool to daydream the specifics on each time and place. As with the Problem-Solution exercise, I learned this from *The Weekend Novelist* by Robert J. Ray.

Note: For some writers, this story boarding tool is the last step they take before writing. For Ezra, it is. For me, I used this tool once, on my first novel. It was useful but painstaking work. Now I skip this step and draft my scenes using a paragraph format because I like to discover the scene's sensory details as I write and edit. If you've never written a novel before, I do recommend using the story boarding tool to think through all of your scenes. If you find it too painful, feel free to skip to the next, and last lesson.

Storyboarding Elements

Readers need to be grounded in the sensory details of your scene. Here are the storyboarding elements you need to brainstorm for each scene.

- Time/and place: Make sure this is one moment or one place.

- Temperature/season: Be specific.

- Lighting/sounds/smells: Be evocative.

- Symbols/images: Let your imagination pull in whatever it wants. Trust what shows up. This can be something tangible in your story or a metaphor used to express an emotion.

- Character/relationships: List all who are "on stage" in the scene.

Dialogue:

- Subjects: What are people speaking about?

- Subtexts: What are they not saying, but only thinking or feeling? Think—Hidden agendas and secrets. These may come across in body language or be completely hidden from the other characters.

Scene Action:

- Large: Think big movements that move the story forward, like stepping out of a car and crossing the street.
- Small: Think micro-movements, facial expressions, and gestures from the characters.

- POV: Point of view. From whose perspective is this scene being revealed?

- Climax: Show the moment of crisis, conflict, or dilemma. Every scene needs one.

- Exit line: What does a character say at the end of the scene? Hook the reader with this so they want to know what happens next. Make them worry.

ACTION

Take twenty to thirty minutes to fill out these elements for each scene. Go here for the Workbook http://bethb.net/bonusworkbook for the Story-boarding Cards to print out.

NEXT

In this last lesson, you're invited to draft a Scene-by-Scene Outline in paragraph format. You can use this exercise as an alternative to the Problem-Solution and story boarding tools, or in addition to them. For me, this is the final step I take before writing my story.

TWENTY

Scene-by-Scene Outline

*T*here are many ways to draft an outline for your story. Some writers use post-it notes on a cork board. Others use spreadsheets. Still others use mind maps or Scrivener, a software for writers. I recommend you try different ways of mapping out your story to find what works for you. Above all, trust yourself. As I shared in the introduction, there is no right way to plan a book, only the way that works for you.

Block off time to do this exercise. The first time I drafted my scene-by-scene outline, it took me about four or five hours. I sat at my favorite cafe and wrote long hand on whatever scraps of paper I had. It was a lot of fun, and scary, in a good way. The subsequent times I've done this exercise, I dictated my thoughts into my iPhone in two to three forty-five-minute sessions, or I typed them directly into Scrivener. As for many writers, my methods evolved as I did—and still do!

As an outline, use the Problem-Solution results you created or your character's fears in your List of 20. I usually just need to know ahead of time my starting incident and the general feeling I want to end the story with, then I just dive in.

Start

Start your scene-by-scene outline by writing the scene number and putting in parentheses the point of view character (POV). Next, draft the external and internal problems in relation to the character's goal, what makes these problems worse, and the dilemma the character faces. Or draft your scene in whatever way that works for you.

Here's an example from my book, *The Volcano Witch*. (I originally wrote this example in 2014. Fast forward to 2017, I transformed these notes into *Henrietta and the Battle of the Horse Mesa*, Book 3 of the *Henrietta The Dragon Slayer* series, now published. Many of these notes made it into my final draft.)

Scene 1: (Paulette)

Paulette is sitting in jail near the castle. She really wants Jaxter, now King Jaxter the Just, to treat her as a friend, and perhaps more, but not as a criminal. She doesn't deserve to be there. She has to get out. Maybe if she masters her wayward fire magic, Jaxter will finally respect her. She has to escape, but how?

SCENE 2: (PAULETTE)

In the middle of the night, Paulette convinces/bribes/seduces/promises (not sure until I write!) the guard to help her and gets out of the jail without raising an alarm, but now needs to find passage off the island. A little bribing does the trick and she finds a boat to hide in. She has no idea who owns the boat, only that it's due to leave on the dawn tides. (*Note:* I may not use this scene since there's no real conflict, but I like knowing what happens.)

SCENE 3: (PAULETTE)

Paulette awakens in the middle of the sea to rough voices and threats of violence among the small crew and realizes she's in a tiny boat with a group of thugs and smugglers. Once ashore, she has to use her fire magic to fend off unwanted advances and threats to sell her into slavery. She escapes into the woods, barely. She only hopes she's going in the right direction: North to find the Volcano Witch in Varangia, the land no one has traveled into in over one hundred years. She hopes the Volcano Witch will help her master her fire magic and finally gain the respect of Jaxter.

. . .

THAT WAS A START! MY GOAL WAS TO DRAFT sixty or seventy scenes in paragraph form, like those above. I know from experience that that's how many scenes I need to craft a 250+ page novel. (If you're curious to see all three novels in this series, they are published and available at many online retailers. More here: http://author.bethbarany.com/ya-fantasy/.)

ACTION

Craft your scene-by-scene outline using the outline in the bonus workbook:

http://bethb.net/bonusworkbook.

NEXT

Now that you've planned your novel, you're ready to write. I have some tips about that in the Next Steps section.

Next Steps: Write Your Novel

"Whatever you can do, or dream you can, begin it. Boldness has genius, power and magic in it."
—William Hutchinson Murray (1913-1996) from his 1951 book *The Scottish Himalayan Expedition* (though often attributed to J.W. von Goethe)

How to Start

Community counts for a lot. Without the various writing groups, associations, and critique groups that Ezra and I have been involved in over the years, we wouldn't have been able to write and publish the novels we have.

What support do you need? What is the next step you will take? How can you set up a structure of accountability and support so that you can do the day-to-day work of writing your novel?

What tools do you need? Such things like software, computers, pens, notebooks. Some of the specialized software tools we use to plan and write: Index Cards for iPad (for Ezra), Scrivener (for Beth and Ezra), Evernote (for Beth).

What environment do you need to write? A quiet house, a busy café, a seaside town?

Here are some steps you can take to start writing your novel:

1. In November, join National Novel Writing Month (NaNoWriMo.org) and take part in the many write-ins organized around the world. In April and July, you can join Camp NaNo challenges in the NaNoWriMo community: https://campnanowrimo.org/.
2. Join a local writer's group or online community, or both.
3. Join a local writer association.
4. Join our annual Write Your Novel support group every November.

Further resources on how to find a critique group and writing associations are in the Bonus section here: http://bethb.net/bonusworkbook.

Resources for Further Reading & Study

Select Courses at Barany School of Fiction

"Craft Compelling Characters,"
    https://school.bethbarany.com/p/compelling-characters

"Plan Your Novel: 30-Day Writing Challenge,"
    https://school.bethbarany.com/p/30daywc

"Edit Your Novel Bootcamp: 30-Day Writing Challenge for Dedicated Novelists,"
    https://school.bethbarany.com/p/edit-your-novel-bootcamp

"How to Choose Your Story's Structure, Learn the ins and outs of five powerful storytelling structures" by Beth Barany and Lynn Johnston, https://school.bethbarany.com/p/how-to-choose-your-story-structure

Introduction

Cron, Lisa. *Wired For Story: The Writer's Guide to Using Brain Science to Hook Readers from the Very First Sentence*, Ten Speed Press, 2012

Sample, Ian. "Neanderthals – not modern humans – were first artists on Earth, experts claim Neanderthals painted on cave walls in Spain 65,000 years ago – tens of thousands of years before modern humans arrived, say researchers" 22 Feb 2018, https://www.theguardian.com/science/2018/feb/22/neanderthals-not-humans-were-first-artists-on-earth-experts-claim

Essential Tips

Coyne, Shawn. *Story Grid: What Great Editors Know*, Black Irish Books, StoryGrid.com, c. 2015

Dixon, Deb. *Goal, Motivation, Conflict, Gryphon Books for Writers*, c. 2001.
www.gryphonbooksforwriters.com

Flippo, Hyde. "A Well Known Quote Attributed to Goethe May Not Be [sic] Actually Be His," Updated

January 21, 2018,
https://www.thoughtco.com/goethe-quote-may-not-be-his-4070881

National Novel Writing Month,
   https://nanowrimo.org/

Resources for Crafting Characters

Buchheit, Carl. *Transformational NLP: A New Psychology*,
White Cloud Press, c. 2017

Card, Orson Scott. *Characters and Viewpoint: Proven advice and timeless techniques for creating compelling characters by an award-winning author*, Writer's Digest Books, c. 2010

Douma, Jesse. "Industry Insider TV Pilot Proposal,"
The Writers Store,
https://desertscreenwritersgroup.files.wordpress.com
/2015/10/tv-pilot-kit-writers-store.pdf

Low, Jon. *Your Brand of Distinction: Earn More Money, Stand Out from the Crowd, Touch the Hearts of Many*, 2nd edition, Fractal Enterprise Pty Ltd, c. 2018

NLP Marin, http://www.nlpmarin.com/

Rasley, Alicia,
http://www.aliciarasley.com/index.php/craft/

Seth, Anil. "Your brain hallucinates your conscious reality," TED2017 | April 2017, https://www.ted.com/talks/anil_seth_how_your_brai n_hallucinates_your_conscious_reality/transcript#t-2847

Simpson, Patricia. Plot Spinner, http://www.patriciasimpson.com/PlotSpinner/ snapsynopsis.aspx

O'Brien, Tim, *The Things They Carried*, Mariner Books, c. 2009

Story Structure Resources

Campbell, Joseph. *The Hero with a Thousand Faces*, Princeton University Press; 21st edition, c. 1973

Hudson, Kim. *The Virgin's Promise: Writing Stories of Feminine Creative, Spiritual, and Sexual Awakening*, Michael Wiese Productions, 2011

McCutcheon, Pam. and Michael Waite, *The Writer's Brainstorming Kit: Thinking in New Directions*, Parker Hayden Media, c. 2016

Monterusso, Rebecca. "Writing Scenes that work" by https://storygrid.com/writing-scenes-work/

Ray, Robert J. *The Weekend Novelist: Learn to Write a Novel in 52 Weeks*, Billboard Books; Revised, Updated edition, c. 2011

Thompson, Lincoln. "37 Books With Plot Twists That Will Blow Your Mind," September 23, 2016, https://www.buzzfeed.com/lincolnthompson/37-books-with-mindblowing-plot-twists

Vogler Christopher. *The Writers Journey: Mythic Structure for Writers*, Michael Wiese Productions; 3rd edition, c. 2007

Software Tools

Evernote, https://www.evernote.com/
Index Cards for iPad, https://www.denvog.com/app/index-card/
Scrivener, https://literatureandlatte.com/

Acknowledgments

Thank you to all the creativity and writing teachers I ever learned from, not mentioned in this book, because your name or book title has faded into subconsciousness and integrated into how I live.

A huge thank you to my partner in life and in this book, Ezra. I couldn't have done it without you, sweetie.

A huge thanks to my early readers: Hugh Tipping, Bonnie Johnston, Jon Low, Mary Van Everbroeck, Ann W. Shannon (big thanks for the Plan Your Novel Scrivener template), Lisa Coughlin, Keri Kruspe, Gary Lea, Arianna Golden, Susan Isola, Cheryl Rider, Brenda D Ballard, Kate Evers, Karilee Wirthlin. And a big thank you to all my students without whom I wouldn't be able to teach this material.

Also by Beth Barany

Overcome Writer's Block

Writer's Adventure Guide

Twitter for Authors

Mastering Deep Point of View (Published by Writer's Fun Zone Publishing)

About the Authors

About Beth Barany

Beth Barany is an award-winning novelist, master neuro-linguistic programming practitioner, and certified creativity coach for writers. She specializes in helping writers experience clarity, so they can write, revise, and proudly publish their novels to the delight of their readers. Her courses are packed with useful hands-on information that you can implement right away. She runs an online school for fiction writers and a 12-month group coaching program to help them get published. More resources on publishing, book marketing, and novel writing are on her blog, Writer's Fun Zone. When she's not helping writers, Beth writes magical tales of romance, mystery, and adventure that empower women and girls to be the heroes of their own lives.

About the Authors

About Ezra Barany

Ezra Barany loves riveting readers with thrillers, but by order of the Department of Motor Vehicles he must place a warning on every book cover, "Do not read while driving." His first two books in *The Torah Codes* series were award-winning international bestsellers. In his free time, he has eye-opening discussions on the art of writing novels with his wife and book coach Beth Barany. A high school physics teacher, Ezra lives in Oakland with his beloved wife and two cats working on the next book in *The Torah Codes* series. Ezra, not the cats. For a free short story in *The Torah Codes* series, "Mourner's Kaddish," go to http://www.thetorahcodes.com/.

Made in the USA
San Bernardino, CA
22 July 2019